The
DHAMMAPADA

Bantam Wisdom Editions

New Translations and Interpretations of Ancient and Sacred Texts

TAO TE CHING:
The Classical Book of Integrity and the Way
Lao Tzu
TRANSLATED BY VICTOR H. MAIR

THE BHAGAVAD-GITA:
Krishna's Counsel in Time of War
TRANSLATED BY BARBARA STOLER MILLER

I CHING:
A New Interpretation for Modern Times
SAM REIFLER

THE BOOK OF FIVE RINGS
MIYAMOTO MUSASHI

A GARDEN BEYOND PARADISE:
The Mystical Poetry of Rumi
TRANSLATED BY JONATHAN STAR AND SHAHRAM SHIVA

NO BARRIER:
Unlocking the Zen Koan
TRANSLATION AND COMMENTARY BY THOMAS CLEARY

THE TIBETAN BOOK OF THE DEAD
TRANSLATED BY ROBERT A. F. THURMAN

WANDERING ON THE WAY:
Early Taoist Tales and Parables of Chuang Tzu
TRANSLATED BY VICTOR H. MAIR

VISIONS OF GOD:
Four Medieval Mystics and Their Writings
KAREN ARMSTRONG

The
DHAMMAPADA
Sayings of Buddha

Translated from the original Pali

Thomas Cleary

BANTAM BOOKS
NEW YORK TORONTO LONDON SYDNEY AUCKLAND

THE DHAMMAPADA

A Bantam Book/January 1995

Library of Congress Cataloging-in-Publication Data

Tipitaka. Suttapitaka. Khuddakanikāya. Dhammapada. English.
    The Dhammapada : sayings of Buddha / translated from the
original Pali by Thomas Cleary.
        p.   cm.
    ISBN 0-553-37376-5
    I. Cleary, Thomas.   II. Title.
    BQ1372.E54C57   1994
    294.3′823—dc20   94-16628
                                                         CIP

Published simultaneously in the United States and Canada

Bantam Books are published by Bantam Books, a division of
Bantam Doubleday Dell Publishing Group, Inc. Its trademark, consisting of the words "Bantam Books" and the
portrayal of a rooster, is Registered in U.S. Patent and
Trademark Office and in other countries. Marca Reg-
istrada. Bantam Books, 1540 Broadway, New York, New
York 10036.

PRINTED IN THE UNITED STATES OF AMERICA

FFG   0 9 8 7 6 5 4 3 2 1

The
DHAMMAPADA

Journey to the Magic City

A PATH TO INNER PEACE

Introduction

The quest for inner peace is one of the most ancient endeavors of humankind. Perhaps an inevitable by-product of consciousness itself, the search for serenity and freedom has occupied outstanding thinkers throughout history. So real and so urgent was the realization of the first thinking humans of their need for inner peace, it would seem, that theories and techniques of mental freedom evolved in ancient societies along with material technologies.

Wen-Tzu, an ancient Chinese book, describes the origin and development of human psychological complications in several stages. At first, "pure simplicity had not yet been lost, so all beings were very relaxed." When society fell away from this pristine state, "there was a dawning of deliberate effort; people were on the verge of leaving their innocent mind and consciously understanding the universe." Eventually "all the people stood straight up and thinkingly bore the burden of looking and listening," and ultimately "people came to relish and desire things, and intelligence was seduced by externals; essential life lost its reality."

An ancient Indian book, *Dasabhumika-isvara,* presents an even more vivid and graphic picture of those mental afflictions infecting humanity that have continued to produce fear, strife, rapine, and all that we consider harmful and undesirable throughout history:

Because of continually slipping
into erroneous views,
because of minds shrouded
by the darkness of ignorance,
because of being puffed up with pride,
because of conceptions,
because of mental fixation
of desires caught in the net of craving,
because of hopes pursued by actions
in the tangle of deceit and falsehood,
because of deeds connected with envy and jealousy
producing mundane states,
because of accumulation of actions
rife with passion, hatred, and folly,
because of the flames of mind
ignited by anger and resentment,

because of undertakings of actions
bound up with delusion,
because of seeds in the mind,
intellect, and consciousness
bound to the flows
of lust, existence, and ignorance.

Countless systems of thought and action were devised by ancient people to counter the ever-more-evident growth of negative by-products of the increasing complexity of the human mind and human societies. The great variety of these systems even included such desperate measures as extreme denial and negation of the ordinary facts of life; many others, though seeming to be less extreme, proved just as futile as denial and negation.

Over centuries, even millennia, countless ways to inner peace were tested, adopted, adapted, and abandoned. Vast literatures, at first orally transmitted, then later written, developed out of this immemorial quest.

One of the most respected of these books is called *Dhammapada,* "statements of principle," a popular collection of sayings on the journey to inner peace from discourses attributed to Gautama Buddha, who lived about five hundred years before Christ. Gautama is believed to have attained perfect peace of mind himself, and also to have then spent forty-nine years traveling from place to place teaching others how to secure serenity and inward freedom as well.

The *Dhammapada* is one of the oldest and most beloved classics of early Buddhism. An anthology of statements of Buddha's teaching (which is what the title means), it is drawn from the ancient Pali Canon, one of the great bodies of primary Buddhist literature. The original text consists of four hundred and twenty-three aphorisms grouped into twenty-six chapters. Known for its simplicity and easy readability, the *Dhammapada* is perhaps the best primer of basic Buddhism to be found anywhere.

According to Buddhist tradition, there were more than sixty different philosophies current in Buddha's time, at least six of which were relatively prominent and well-known. Although he addressed forest ascetics and village citizenry as well as nobles, grandees, and priests in terms common in the culture of the time, the Buddha neither accepted the authority of tradition nor subscribed to any of the speculative views of the new era. Redefining central concepts of ethics and spirituality, the Buddha produced a unique teaching that was not simply an outgrowth of its cultural milieu, nor yet an isolated anomaly or counterculture.

The Buddha did not teach by ritual or dogma, denying that these lead to freedom and enlightenment. He repudiated the ancient Aryan caste system, which had originated in the remote past as a labor division device but had become oppressive under later Aryan imperialism. Buddha also abandoned the cultish ceremonialism of the ancient priesthood; giving up the arcane hieratic language of the Brahmin priests, he talked to people from all walks of life in local vernacular.

The Buddha's individual breakthrough in the already sophisticated praxis and psychology of yoga, unparalleled even in such an atmosphere of intense spiritual endeavor, is one of his greatest achievements. Entire groups of yogis and ascetics are known to have abandoned their own occult observances and entered Buddhist discipleship en masse, drawn to the perfect calm and clarity of the Buddha's way.

The Buddha's teachings were never compiled into one uniform tradition, but there appear to have been two main streams, each itself highly variegated. A stream of vernacular oral tradition was passed on among mendicants, while a broader and more diverse written tradition, which nonetheless included the quintessential teachings of the oral tradition, was passed on by people known as *Dharmadhara* or Holders of Teaching.

The oral tradition was eventually written down using Pali, a newly developed literary language based on regularization of the vernaculars used by the Buddha, his disciples, and the early Buddhists in various communities. The many discourses of Buddha in this oral tradition beautifully illustrate the profound serenity and unalterable dignity of this religion of peace. The focus of the teachings is the mastery and purification of the self, strength and sobriety of character, and the ultimate attainment of freedom and independence.

In the context of the totality of Buddhism, the process of individual liberation and peace of mind outlined in the teachings of the *Dhammapada* is referred to as the Lesser Journey, while its goal of nirvana is called the Magic City. From there, a new perspective opens up; this is the Great Journey, whose goal of enlightened knowledge and vision is called the Land of Treasures. Once in that realm of consciousness, the ultimate journey is revealed; this is called the Tantra or Fundamental Continuity, wherein heaven and earth are united.

The final completion of the journey, and the soundness of the spiritual state of the traveler, depend on the insight, serenity, and forbearance acquired in the course of the Lesser Journey. Those who attempt to undertake the Greater Journey or the Fundamental

Continuity without the spiritual and moral provisions accumulated on the Lesser Journey imperil themselves and those around them, stagnating just as surely as those who stop along the way.

According to the *Saddharmapundarika-sutra,* when the Buddha first announced the Greater Journey, and revealed the preparatory role of the Lesser Journey, a large number of people who thought they had already attained ultimate salvation left the assembly in a huff. Although this is a representation, history confirms that there have been, since early times, factions of followers who refused the teachings of the Greater Journey and remained attached to their own interpretation of nirvana as the highest goal. Because they interpreted the Lesser Journey in isolation, therefore, they developed views and practices that proved, from the point of view of the Greater Journey, to be sterile and even morbid.

This present translation and presentation of Buddha's teachings from the famous *Dhammapada* on the way to inner peace has been done from the point of view of the Greater Journey, restoring the original balance found in the overall context of Buddhism and dropping the priggishness and pessimism commonly projected on the Buddhism of the Lesser Journey, past and present, by those who consider it in isolation as something in, of, and for itself. For the convenience of the reader, each chapter is preceded by a brief translator's orientation and punctuated by translator's notes and comments.

I. Couplets

THIS FIRST CHAPTER PRESENTS ITS TEACHING in sets of verses contrasting good and bad ways and their consequences, juxtaposing the causes of joy and sorrow. Purity of mind, self-control, moderation, freedom from rancor, accurate thought, purity of action, and practical application are praised as good ways in contrast to corruption of mind, grudge bearing, hatred, laziness, self-indulgence, false thinking, tainted action, and heedlessness.

1. Everything has mind in the lead, has mind in the forefront, is made by mind.
   If one speaks or acts with a corrupt mind, misery will follow, as the wheel of a cart follows the foot of the ox.

2. Everything has mind in the lead, has mind in the forefront, is made by mind. If one speaks or acts with a pure mind, happiness will follow, like a shadow that never leaves.

The Buddhist **Mahaparinirvana-sutra,** *or Scripture of the Absolute Nirvana, says, "Be master of mind, do not be mastered by mind."*

---

3. "He reviled me; he injured me; he defeated me; he deprived me." In those who harbor such grudges, hatred never ceases.
4. "He reviled me; he injured me; he defeated me; he deprived me." In those who do not harbor such grudges, hatred eventually ceases.

The Buddhist **Sandhinirmocana-sutra,** *or Scripture Unlocking the Mysteries, explains that delusion arises from clinging to an imaginary reality formulated under the influence of the "lull of words," the habit-forming influence that repetition of mental talk has on the state of the perceiving and thinking mind.*

---

5. Hatreds do not ever cease in this world by hating, but by not hating; this is an eternal truth.

A Zen Buddhist proverb says, "The arousal of thoughts is sickness; not continuing them is medicine."

6. Others do not know we must pass away here; but
   for those who know this, contention thereby ceases.

Contemplation of impermanence is traditionally recommended
as one of the easiest ways to arouse the inspiration and will for
liberation and enlightenment.

7. One who lives as though the things of the world
   were pure, with senses unguarded and appetite im-
   moderate, lazy and weak, will be overpowered by
   bedevilment, like a weak tree blown over by the
   wind.

Bedevilment is commonly spoken of in Buddhist tradition as
being of four major types:

a) *bedevilment by afflictions (the six major afflictions being*
   greed, hatred, delusion, conceit, doubt, and arbitrary
   opinion)
b) *bedevilment by form, sensation, conception, action, and*
   consciousness
c) *bedevilment by death*
d) *bedevilment by manipulation of sense experience*

8. One who lives as though the things of the world
   are impure, with senses guarded and appetite
   moderate, faithful and diligent, will not be overpowered by bedevilment, like a rock mountain
   unshaken by the wind.
9. One who would wear the saffron robe while not

free from impurity is lacking in self-control and is
not genuine, thus unworthy of the saffron robe.

The saffron robe was a symbol of the Buddhist renunciant,
who would gather discarded rags, wash them, sew them to-
gether into a covering for the body, and dye it a uniform color.
Evidently the saffron robe was in Buddha's time already being
used hypocritically as a kind of camouflage.

---

10. One who has vomited out all filth and concen-
    trates on moral practices has self-control and is
    genuine, thus is worthy of the saffron robe.
11. Those who think the unreal is real and see the real
    as unreal do not reach the real, being in the realm
    of false thinking.
12. Those who know the real is real and see the un-
    real as unreal arrive at the real, being in the
    realm of accurate thought.

Accurate perception and accurate thinking are both elements
of the Eightfold Path recommended by Buddha for the realiza-
tion of liberation.

---

13. As rain leaks into a poorly roofed house, so does
    passion invade an uncultivated mind.
14. As no rain leaks into a well-roofed house, passion
    does not invade a cultivated mind.

Buddhist texts commonly use the image of guarding or protecting the mind, preventing the invasion of influences that render it vulnerable to delusion and compulsion.

15. One who does evil sorrows in this world and after death, sorrowful in both. Seeing the pollution of one's own actions, one is tormented by sorrow and grief.

16. One who does good is happy in this world and after death, happy in both. Seeing the purity of one's own actions, one is happy, most joyful.

17. One who does evil suffers regret in this world and after death, suffering regret in both. One suffers regret knowing one has done wrong, and suffers even more when gone to a state of misery.

18. One who does good rejoices in this world and after death, joyful in both. One rejoices knowing one has done good, and rejoices even more when gone to a state of felicity.

Buddhists consider it axiomatic that we individually and collectively experience the results of our own individual and collective actions; Buddhist concepts of morality and responsibility are based on this law of causality.

19. Even if one talks a lot about what is beneficial, if one does not put it into practice, one is

negligent, like a herder counting the livestock of others; one has no share in spirituality.

20. Even if one speaks little of what is beneficial, one who acts on truth is truthful; having abandoned lust, hatred, and folly, endowed with accurate insight, liberated in mind, unattached to this world or the next, one has a share in spirituality.

The **Avatamsaka-sutra,** *or Flower Ornament Scripture, likens those who do not practice what they preach to penurious accountants, deaf musicians, and blind artists.*

II. Vigilance

THIS CHAPTER FOCUSES PARTICULARLY ON describing the merits of vigilance and rebuking negligence and heedlessness. Vigilance means exercising unremitting awareness of self, truth, and reality, sloughing off the torpor of heedlessness to act practically on realities.

1. Vigilance is the realm of immortality; negligence is the realm of death. People who are vigilant do not die; people who are negligent are as if dead.

   The vigilant ones "do not die" because they are attuned to objective reality, which is eternal; not fixated on subjective delusion, which is temporal.

2. The wise, with thorough knowledge of vigilance,
   enjoy being vigilant and delight in the realm of
   the noble.

In Buddhist language, nobility refers to attainment of charac-
ter and wisdom rather than inheritance of status by birth.

---

3. Meditative, persevering, always striving diligently,
   the wise attain nirvana, supreme peace.

Nirvana (Pali nibbana) means "extinction," meaning the ex-
tinction of afflictions (such as the aforementioned greed, ha-
tred, delusion, conceit, doubt, and arbitrary opinion). The
Sandhinirmocana-sutra *refers to "quiescent nirvana" as*
"the highest expedient." It is also called the nectar or ambrosia
of immortality, the elixir that makes the infinite endlessness of
the Greater Journey bearable to the individual human mind.

---

4. Energetic, alert, pure in deed, careful in action,
   self-controlled, living in accord with truth, the
   vigilant one will rise in repute.
5. By energy, vigilance, self-control, and self-
   mastery, the wise one may make an island that a
   flood cannot sweep away.
6. Fools, unintelligent people, indulge in heedlessness. The wise one, however, guards vigilance as
   the best of riches.
7. Do not indulge in negligence, do not be intimate

with attachment to desire. The vigilant one, meditative, gains great happiness.

8. When the sage expels negligence by vigilance, climbing the tower of insight, the wise one, sorrowless, gazes upon the sorrowing, ignorant crowd below, as one on a mountain peak views people on the ground.

Buddhists on the Greater Journey are always warned to avoid becoming so intoxicated by the state described here as to lose pity and compassion for others. That proscribed intoxication is called the Deep Pit of Liberation.

---

9. Vigilant among the heedless, awake among the sleeping, the wise one goes ahead like a racehorse outstripping a nag.

10. Indra became highest of the deified by vigilance. Vigilance they praise; negligence is always censured.

11. The mendicant who delights in vigilance, fearing negligence, goes along like a fire burning up bondage subtle and gross.

12. The mendicant who delights in vigilance, fearing negligence, cannot fall away, being near to nirvana already.

III. Mind

THIS CHAPTER IS A COLLECTION OF SAYINGS
on the mercurial nature of the mind that has
not been stabilized, and on the need for
stabilization of mind in order to sustain cog-
nition of truth. Stabilization is cultivated by
watchfully guarding the mind to keep it from
becoming fragmented by random thoughts;
this watchfulness is cultivated by recollection
of the consequences, good and ill, proceed-
ing from care and negligence in matters of
mental hygiene.

1. The mind is restless, unsteady, hard to
   guard, hard to control. The wise one
   makes it straight, like a fletcher
   straightens an arrow.

2. Like a fish out of water, cast on dry ground, this mind flops around trying to escape the realm of bedevilment.

3. The mind is mercurial, hard to restrain, alighting where it wishes. It is good to master this mind; a disciplined mind brings happiness.

4. Let the wise one watch over the mind, so hard to perceive, so artful, alighting where it wishes; a watchfully protected mind brings happiness.

5. The mind travels afar, acts alone, is incorporeal, and haunts a cave; those who will control it escape the bonds of bedevilment.

The mind "haunts a cave" in the sense of clinging to the body as self and holding to the subjective worldview as the world itself.

---

6. For the wakeful one whose mind is unimpassioned, whose thoughts are undisturbed, who has given up both virtue and sin, there is no fear.

Giving up both virtue and sin means abandoning impulse to evil and relinquishing anticipation of reward for goodness. The Japanese Zen master Bunan warned that when some people hear about detachment from good and evil, they think it means doing evil and thinking that's good.

---

7. Knowing the body to be like a water pitcher, making the mind like a citadel, fight bedevilment with

the weapon of insight. Guard what you have won,
without attachment to it.

---

*Attachment to spiritual attainments is also a source of bond-
age. The classical Zen master Baizhang refers to this as
"affliction by the dust of religion." A Zen proverb says, "The
spoils of war are lost in celebration."*

8. This body, alas, will soon lie on the ground,
   without consciousness, abandoned like a useless
   piece of rotten wood.
9. Whatever an enemy may do to an enemy, and
   whatever the hateful may do to the hateful, the
   mind with a warped intent does even worse than
   that.

---

*The underlying idea here is that ordinarily people readily fear
harm from others without giving equal consideration to how
much they harm themselves.*

10. What not even a mother, a father, or any other
    relative will do, a rightly directed mind does do,
    even better.

---

*Similarly, the underlying idea here is that ordinarily people
readily depend on others for their well-being without giving
equal consideration to what they need to do, or should be
doing, for themselves. Compassion for others is useless if you
cannot first master your own life.*

IV. Flowers

THE TITLE OF THIS CHAPTER STANDS FOR things of the world, which we may heedlessly pursue as vanities even as time and death stalk us, or we may mindfully use constructively to beautify the world if we realize their value. Even better than worldly color and fragrance, the aphorisms go on, is fineness of character, by which one may become, as it is said, like an exquisite lotus growing from a heap of dust.

1. Who will conquer this earth, and this world of death, with its gods? Who will gather well-expressed words of truth, as an expert gathers flowers?

2. It is the studious who will conquer this earth, and the world of death with its gods. It is the studious who will gather well-expressed words of truth, as an expert gathers flowers.

"Studious" in this context does not mean academic studiousness, but sincerity and diligence in studying what is true.

3. Knowing the body is like froth, realizing it is insubstantial, breaking the flowery arrow of the Killer, one goes to a realm invisible to the King of Death.

The Killer is bedevilment personified. See the list on page 9. The King of Death is a personification of death itself in reference to the force of the death process that exacts "payment" of "debts" incurred in life, in the inconceivably intensified perceptual and emotional experience of the end of physical life.

4. Death carries off someone absorbed in picking flowers, just as a flood sweeps away a sleeping village.
5. Death overpowers one absorbed in picking flowers, before one has attained one's aim.

"Picking flowers" here means indulging in objects of desire to the point of becoming heedless of the objective nature of desire.

6. Just as the bee takes the nectar and leaves without damaging the color or scent of the flowers, so should the sage act in a village.

This popular Buddhist image refers to living in the world without obsessions, not bending it out of shape by greedy and aggressive attitudes and behaviors.

7. Do not look at the faults of others, or what others have done or not done; observe what you yourself have done and have not done.

The famous Zen master Dahui used to recommend a parallel proverb as a convenient way to gain access to awakening: "Don't ride another's horse, don't draw another's bow, don't mind another's business."

8. Like a beautiful flower that is colorful but has no fragrance, even well-spoken words bear no fruit in one who does not put them into practice.
9. Like a beautiful flower that is both colorful and also fragrant, well-spoken words bear fruit in one who puts them into practice.
10. Just as many kinds of garlands can be made from a heap of flowers, so also much good can be done by a mortal being.

So much for the popular cliché that Buddhism is pessimistic, negative, or world denying. The Third Chinese Patriarch of

Zen wrote, "Do not despise the six senses, for the six senses are not bad; after all they are the same as true awakening."

11. The scent of flowers does not go against the wind; not sandalwood, not aloes wood, nor jasmine. But the scent of the virtuous does go against the wind; the fragrance of righteousness perfumes all directions.

12. Sandalwood, aloes wood, blue lotus, great-flowered jasmine—even among such fragrant things, the fragrance of virtuous conduct is best of all.

13. The fragrance of aloes wood and sandalwood is but slight; the fragrance of virtuous people is supreme, reaching even to the gods.

The visionary Buddhist scripture **Avatamsaka-sutra** *abounds with images of fragrances symbolizing the "perfume" of morality and goodness of character.*

14. There is no way for bedevilment to assail people who have perfected virtuous conduct, who live vigilantly, and who are liberated by true knowledge.

Apropos of "liberation by true knowledge," the classical Zen master Linji said, "People who study Buddhism should seek real true perception and understanding for now. If you attain real true perception and understanding, then birth and death don't affect you; you are free to go or stay." He also said, "It is most urgent that you seek real true perception and understanding so you can be free in the world and not confused by ordinary spiritualists."

15–16. Just as a fragrant, delightful lotus grows from
        a heap of dust thrown on the road, so also in
        the midst of blind mortals, who are like so
        much dust, do disciples of the truly enlight-
        ened shine.

A similar image of "being in the world but not of the world" is used to describe the Greater Journey, in which individual liberation and enlightenment are continually "reinvested" in the world for the benefit of people of the world.

V. The Fool

THIS CHAPTER DEALS WITH THE MENTAL POISON of folly, one of the factors known to produce misery. Here the fool is characterized by ignorance of truth, possessiveness, conceit, insensitivity, shortsightedness, and self-importance. Great emphasis is placed on the fact that the company of fools is not merely wasteful but even injurious; fools hurt not only themselves but others as well, through ignorance and misapplied knowledge.

1. The night is long to the wakeful, a distance of ten miles is long to the weary; the road of life and death is long to fools who do not know the truth.

2. A wayfarer who does not find anyone better or
   equal should firmly go alone; there is no companionship with a fool.

_____

The companionship of fools is harmful even in the absence of
ill intentions; the good will of a fool can be as harmful,
through ignorant action, as the opposition of a fool.

_____

3. "I have sons, I have wealth"—the fool suffers
   thinking thus. Even one's self is not one's own;
   how then sons, how then wealth?

_____

The Qur'an says, "Vying for more and more diverts you until
you go to the tombs." Also, "Know that the life of the world is
but diversion and distraction, ostentation and vying for glory
among yourselves, and striving for more and more wealth and
children. . . . And what is the life of the world but the stuff of
deception?"

_____

4. A fool who is conscious of his folly is thereby
   wise; the fool who thinks himself wise is the one
   to be called a fool.

_____

Confucius said, "Shall I teach you how to know something?
Realize you know it when you know it, and realize you don't
know it when you don't."

5. Even if a fool associates with someone wise all his life, he will never know the truth, just as a spoon cannot discern the taste of the soup.

The kind of "pearls before swine" situation described by this aphorism is commonly represented in folk expressions such as "the name of the Buddha in the ear of a horse" and "a piece of gold to a cat."

---

6. Someone who is intelligent will realize the truth right away by associating with someone wise for even a while, just as the tongue discerns the taste of the soup.

---

*The **Mahaparinirvana-sutra** describes those quick to learn as like good horses that set off at the mere shadow of the crop, not needing to be whipped or spurred. There are many examples of Hindu philosophers, ascetics, and yogis attaining liberation very quickly through the penetrating answers of Buddha to their questions and challenges. See aphorisms 15 and 16.*

---

7. Stupid fools act as enemies to themselves, doing evil deeds that have painful results.
8. No deed is well done that is followed by regret, whose consequences are attended by tears and weeping.
9. That deed is well done that is not followed by regret, whose consequences are attended by joy and happiness.

Far from being irrational and mysterious, as some pseudo-Zen "masters" would have it, Buddhism requires common sense and clear thinking.

10. As long as it has not borne fruit, the fool thinks evil sweet; but when evil bears fruit, then the fool suffers misery.

11. The abstinence of the ignorant is worth less than a sixteenth part of those who have integrated all truths.

Hadrat Ali, the fourth orthodox Caliph of Islam, is reported to have said, "How many of those who fast have nothing to their fast but hunger and thirst!"

12. The effect of an evil deed, like milk, does not congeal at once; it follows the foolish one, burning like fire covered with ashes.

According to Buddhist philosophy, actions bear fruit in different time frames; a result does not necessarily follow immediately upon its cause. Those who do not keep this in mind may inadvertently misperceive the true cause of a given event.

13–14. Whatever knowledge a fool acquires tends to be harmful; it destroys the fool's virtue, going to his head: He may wish for undeserved honor, precedence among mendicants, rulership among settled populations, and homage among other groups.

Combine the Western proverbs "Knowledge is power" and "Power corrupts" and see what you get.

One of the strangest ideas to be found among Western Buddhist groups is that the greater number of males accorded recognition, honor, precedence, or rulership in Buddhist historical annals means that females were suppressed in Asian Buddhism. Using the logic of Buddhist teaching itself, as illustrated here, in contrast, this phenomenon may simply mean that more male fools acquired knowledge.

---

15. "This I have done; let the laity and the mendicants know of it! In what is to be done and what is not to be done, let my will be followed!" Such are the thoughts of fools; thus do craving and conceit grow.

16. One is the way to gain, the other is the way to nirvana; knowing this fact, students of Buddha should not take pleasure in being honored, but should practice detachment.

VI. The Wise

THIS CHAPTER PRESENTS THE COUNTERPOINT
to the fool described in the fifth chapter. Here
the technique of making a point by compari-
son and contrast introduced in the opening
chapter of Couplets is pursued from one
chapter to the next. A descriptive rebuke of
the fool is followed by illustrative praise of the
wise. The wise, says the Buddha, are not those
who are loved by all, but those who speak and
live the truth; that is why they are not liked by
all people, but are liked by the good and disliked by the bad. The wise are masters of
themselves, not moved by the opinions of
others, clear-minded, peaceful, principled,
independent, free from compulsion. Such
people are said to attain perfect nirvana, con-
summate peace of mind, even in this world.

1. Whoever sees one who points out faults as a revealer of hidden treasures should follow such a wise one, intelligent, who tells what is blameworthy. Good, not ill, happens to one who follows such an individual.

The great Zen master Wuzu said, "The ancients were glad to hear of their own errors."

2. Let one admonish and educate, and lead away from what is uncouth; then one will be liked by good people and disliked by bad people.

Confucius said, "It is better when the good among the people like you and the bad dislike you."

3. One should not associate with evil companions, one should not associate with base companions. Associate with good companions, associate with noble companions.

In his famous **Admonitions**, the classical Zen master Guishan wrote, "Companionship with the good is like walking through dew and mist; although they do not drench your clothing, in time it becomes imbued with moisture. Familiarity with the evil increases wrong knowledge and views, day and night creating evil."

4. Those who delight in truth sleep peacefully, with clear minds. The wise always take pleasure in truth expounded by the noble.

Taoists say that ancient sages "slept without dreams and rose without worries."

---

5. The irrigation engineer guides water, the fletcher makes arrows true, the carpenter makes timber straight; the wise master themselves.

The **Tao Te Ching** *says, "Those who overcome others are powerful; those who overcome themselves are strong."*

---

6. As a solid boulder does not shake in the wind, the wise are not moved by censure or praise.

The Taoist Huainan Masters say, "Sages are not controlled by names."

---

7. Just as a deep lake is clear and clean, so do the wise become clear after hearing the truths.
8. Real people are unattached wherever they are; those at peace do not speak out of desire for pleasure. Whether they encounter comfort or pain, the wise show neither elation nor depression.

The Huainan Masters also say, "When you truly understand human nature and destiny, kindness and justice are naturally included; ups and downs cannot disturb your mind."

9. One should not hope for children, riches, or dominion for oneself or for others. One who does not seek personal enrichment by unrighteous means is ethical, insightful, principled.

This does not mean rejection of the world, but trust in nature and following natural laws of cause and effect.

10. Few are the people who reach the Beyond; the others run along this shore.

"This shore" means the mundane world; the Beyond in this context means nirvana, inner peace.

11. When truth is correctly explained, those who follow truth will go beyond the domain of death, which is so hard to cross over.

Nirvana is also called **amrta,** *which means immortality, or, figuratively, the elixir of immortality.*

12. The wise should abandon evil things and do what is good, leaving attachments and entering into a

life without attachment, the individualism that is
hard to enjoy.

_____

*Life without attachment is true individualism in that it is
tantamount to freedom from "peer pressure." Confucius said,
"Ideal people can stand alone without fear and leave society
without distress."*

_____

13. Let the wise seek enjoyment therein, having given
up all desire, and having rid oneself of mental
pollution.

_____

*"Therein" means the true individualism of life without at-
tachment. It is "hard to enjoy" in the sense that it does not
offer sentimental support for ego and personality satisfactions.*

_____

14. Those in whom the mind is correctly cultivated in
the limbs of perfect enlightenment, who have no
attachments and enjoy being free from grasping,
and who have stopped all compulsion, attain perfect nirvana here in this world.

_____

*The "limbs of enlightenment" are seven in number: 1) recollec-
tion, 2) examination of realities, 3) diligence, 4) joyfulness,
5) tranquillity, 6) concentration, 7) equanimity.*

VII. The Worthy

THIS CHAPTER DESCRIBES THE *ARHAT*, ONE who has completed the Lesser Journey and attained the inner peace of nirvana. The Arhat is said to have no sorrow, no baggage, no compulsive routines, no mental or physical agitation, and no superstition. Dispassionate, serene, they attain liberation and become free.

1. For those who have completed their journey, left sorrow behind, are free in all circumstances, and liberated from all bondage, affliction does not exist.
2. The thoughtful exert themselves; they do not relish attachment. Like swans leaving a lake, they abandon one attachment after another.

3. Those who have no accumulation, who eat with perfect knowledge, whose sphere is emptiness, signlessness, and liberation, are hard to track, like birds in the sky.

To "have no accumulation" means not having a load of psychological "baggage" or "complexes" accumulated in the course of experience in the world.

---

4. Those whose compulsions are gone, who are not attached to food, whose sphere is emptiness, signlessness, and liberation, are hard to track, like birds in the sky.

In the Greater Journey, emptiness, signlessness, and liberation are called the Three Great Meditations. In their objective senses, they are a "sphere," referring to the ultimate truth of realities as inconceivable, not what we imagine, in terms of our subjective attributions, definitions, and attachments.

In Zen Buddhism, the "bird's track" is sometimes used to represent the first stage of Zen practice. Zen master Shigetsu explains, "This path means first getting rid of clinging to self even while living in the present heap of energy and matter, attaining our original state of egolessness. Then you must also know that things have no inherent identities either. Once you realize the selflessness of persons and things, even in the midst of your daily activities you walk in emptiness. This is called traveling the bird's path."

5. Those whose senses are tranquil, like a horse well controlled by a charioteer, who are free from pride and have no compulsions, are the envy of even the gods.

6. For one who is docile as the earth, a pillar of good conduct, like an unpolluted lake, there are no more compulsive routines.

7. The thought is calm, the speech and action are calm, in one who is liberated and gone to serenity by perfect knowledge.

8. The best person is one who is not credulous, who knows the uncreated, who has cut off ties, gotten rid of chance, and renounced desires.

It seems to be easy, and perilous, to confuse credulousness with faith, humility, sincerity, or similar faculties. False teachers, of course, encourage this confusion rather than clarify it. The uncreated is that into which no human artifice enters. To "cut off ties, get rid of chance, and renounce desires" sounds like asceticism, but this is a superficial interpretation. The meaning on the Greater Journey is living in the world through free will in a very special sense, rather than by habit, or willy-nilly, or expectantly.

---

9. Village or forest, hill or dale, anywhere that saints dwell is pleasant.

When Hadrat Ali heard a man reviling the world, he asked, "Are you accusing the world, or is the world accusing you?"

10. Forests are pleasant where people do not frolic;
    those who are free of passion will enjoy them,
    because they are not pleasure seekers.

Buddhist contemplatives on the right path draw a strict line between spiritual resort to forests and aesthetic and recreational resort to forests. The differences in consequences can be seen both in the effects on the individuals and the effects on the environment.

VIII. Thousands

THIS CHAPTER IS GENERALLY AIMED AT DRAW-
ing a distinction between quantity and quality in life, contrasting superficial activities,
observances, and aims with deeper apprecia-
tion of perennial truths and enduring values.

1. Better than a thousand sayings composed of meaningless statements is a
   single meaningful statement on hearing
   which one becomes calm.
2. Better than a thousand verses composed
   of meaningless lines is a single line of
   verse on hearing which one becomes
   calm.

3. Better than one who recites a hundred verses of meaningless lines is one verse on hearing which one becomes calm.

Real Buddhist literature is supposed to be **functional,** *in the instrumental sense of being liberative and enlightening. Aesthetic or other literary concerns are subordinate to the purpose of specific functional application.*

---

4. Though one defeats a million men in battle, one who overcomes the self alone is in fact the highest victor.

5–6. For one who is self-controlled and always disciplined in action, victory over the self is better than victory over others. The victory of someone like this cannot be made into defeat, even by a god, an angel, or a devil.

The Taoist Huainan Masters say, "I do not let the changes of a given time determine the way I master myself. What I call self-mastery means that my nature and life abide where they are secure."

---

7. Even if someone performs ritual sacrifices a thousand times every month for a hundred years, if he honors a self-cultivated individual for even a moment, that honor is better than what is sacrificed in a hundred years.

8. Even if one tends a ceremonial fire in the forest

for a hundred years, if one honors a self-cultivated individual for even a moment, that honor is better than the sacrifice of a hundred years.

9. Whatever may be sacrificed or offered up for a year in this world in order to gain merit, all of that is less than a fourth as good as paying respect to upright people.

As these last three sayings illustrate, the Buddha abandoned cultism, superstition, and ignorant ritualism.

10. For those who are always courteous and respectful of elders, four things increase: life, beauty, happiness, and strength.

This does not represent a primitive or superstitious doctrine of reward for good deeds on the model of a commercial transaction. Courtesy and respect for elders encourage respect for life and living beings; these feelings have a calming and focusing effect on the mind and body, which naturally enhance the general health and well-being of the individual who behaves in this manner as well as the group or community in which this habit prevails.

---

11. It is better to live one day ethically and reflectively than to live a hundred years immoral and unrestrained.
12. It is better to live one day wisely and reflectively

than to live a hundred years in ignorance and indulgence.

13. It is better to live one day making strenuous effort than to live a hundred years lazily and
listlessly.

14. It is better to live one day seeing transitoriness
than to live a hundred years not seeing transitoriness.

---

*Awareness of impermanence enhances your experience of the
world, sharpening your sense of the uniqueness of the moment
and its opportunity.*

---

15. It is better to live one day seeing the deathless
state than to live a hundred years not seeing the
deathless state.

---

*Seeing the deathless state (nirvana) ever-present behind the
shifting scenes of the world gives you the ultimate equanimity
to see what is what in this world while simultaneously bearing
the realization of what is ultimately and finally real and true.*

---

16. It is better to live one day seeing the ultimate
truth than to live a hundred years not seeing the
ultimate truth.

IX. Evil

THIS CHAPTER EMPHASIZES THE INEVITABILITY of ill consequences following evil actions. This inevitability, it must be emphasized, does not mean inevitable immediacy; depending on the totality of contributing conditions, there may be a time lag of any duration between an action and the ripening of its consequences. This is precisely the reason for reminders and warnings like those found in the aphorisms of this chapter; if the ill consequences of evil acts were inevitably immediate, there would be no further need for admonition. Similarly, the development of bad behavioral habits may be too insidious for the individual to consider ill consequences in time to avoid them, if not for deliberate reflection.

1. Hasten to do good, restrain your mind from evil.
   The mind of one who is sluggish about doing
   good finds amusement in evil.
2. Whoever has done something wrong should not
   repeat it; do not set your mind on it, for misery
   is an accumulation of evil.
3. Let those who have done good repeat it again and
   again; set your mind on it, for happiness is the
   accumulation of good.

---

*Even in the Lesser Journey, whose goal is peace, it is necessary
to engage in constructive and positive action in order to bring
about individual development of the capacity for liberated
knowledge and vision.*

---

4. Even one who is evil sees good as long as the evil
   has not developed; but when the evil has developed, the evildoer sees evils.
5. Even one who is good may see ill as long as the
   good has not developed; but when the good has
   developed, the good one sees good.

---

*The time lapse that may occur between specific causes and
their effects creates latitude for all sorts of imaginative self-
deception.*

---

6. Do not underestimate evil, thinking it will not affect you. Dripping water can even fill a pitcher,

drop by drop; a fool is filled with evil, even if
one accumulates it little by little.

The **Tao Te Ching** *says, "No calamity is greater than under-estimating opponents."*

7. Do not underestimate good, thinking it will not
   affect you. Dripping water can even fill a pitcher,
   drop by drop; one who is wise is filled with
   good, even if one accumulates it little by little.

The **Tao Te Ching** *says, "Do the great while it is still small."*

8. Just as a merchant with many goods but few
   companions avoids a dangerous road, and just as
   someone who wants to live avoids poison, one
   should avoid all evils.

*The classical Zen master Caoshan presented the image of
walking through a village where the wells are all poisoned.
The Japanese Zen master Dogen wrote, "When studying in
this way, evils are manifest as a continuum of being ever not
done. Inspired by this manifestation, seeing through to the
fact that evils are not done, one settles it finally. At precisely
such a time, as the beginning, middle, and end manifest as
evils not done, evils are not born from conditions, they are only
not done; evils do not perish through conditions, they are only
not done."*

9. One without a wound on the hand may remove poison by hand; the poison will not get in where there is no wound. There is no evil for one who does none.

10. If anyone offends an innocent person, the ill of that will come back to that fool, like dust thrown into the wind.

11. Some are born in the womb; evildoers go to hell. People whose conduct is good go to heaven; people who are free from compulsion attain nirvana.

Nirvana is even finer than the happiness of heaven.

12. There is nowhere in the world—not in the sky, nor in the sea, nor in the depths of the earth— where one can escape evil deeds.

13. There is nowhere in the world—not in the sky, nor in the sea, nor in the depths of the earth— where death will not overcome you.

There is nowhere one can escape the consequences of one's own actions, or the operation of natural laws of causality. These lines not only express evident truths, they also indirectly repudiate all beliefs that have only distraction value.

X. Violence

THIS CHAPTER FOCUSES ON DEVELOPMENT OF compassion for others by thinking of them in the same way one thinks of oneself. Based on this realization, the aphorisms in this chapter encourage nonviolence and protection of others by self-control. For those who confuse self-control with self-mortification, this chapter also includes a warning about the futility of mechanical asceticism and the need for real inner transformation of character rather than mere outward change of habit or appearance.

1. Everyone trembles at the whip, everyone is afraid of death. Considering others as yourself, do not kill or promote killing.

2. Everyone trembles at the whip; everyone likes life. Considering others as yourself, do not kill or promote killing.
3. Whoever hurts living beings—who all want happiness—may be seeking personal happiness, but will not attain felicity after death.
4. Whoever does not hurt living beings—who all seek happiness—though seeking personal happiness, will attain felicity after death.

Compassion is ordinarily considered to be the distinguishing hallmark of the Buddhism of the Greater Journey, but as illustrated here in the first four aphorisms of this chapter, it is also part of the Lesser Journey, because it is a natural consequence of perceiving material laws.

5. Do not say anything harsh; what you have said will be said back to you. Angry talk is painful; retaliation will get you.
6. If you can make yourself as still as a broken gong, you have attained nirvana; there is no agitation in you.

Zen master Dogen recommends meditation on the proverb, "If you can keep your mouth as silent as your nose, you will avoid a lot of trouble."

---

7. As a cowherd drives cattle to pasture with a rod, so do old age and death drive the life of the living.

8. But the fool doing evil deeds does not understand; the idiot burns by his own acts, as though he were on fire.

9–12. Whoever injures the innocent and offends the upright quickly goes to one of ten certain states: discomfort, loss, physical injury, serious illness, insanity, oppression by a ruler, cruel slander, loss of relations, destruction of possessions, or fire burns his houses. When his body dissolves, the fool is born in hell.

13. Neither nudism nor matted hair, nor wearing mud nor fasting, nor lying on hard ground, nor dust and dirt, nor squatting motionless will purify a mortal who has not gotten over doubt and desire.

Hadrat Ali said, "Sleep in certainty is better than prayer in doubt."

---

14. If one practices equanimity even if adorned, if one is peaceful, restrained, disciplined, and chaste, that is the one who is priestly, the one who is religious, the one who is a mendicant.

"Even if adorned" means "even though living an outwardly ordinary life in the world." Ideals of priestliness and abstinence were redefined and refocused by Gautama Buddha to refer to inner qualities rather than outward performances.

15. Is there anyone in the world restrained by modesty, who does not arouse censure, as a good horse needs no whipping?

16. Like a good horse on whom a whip alights, be earnest and energetic. By faith, discipline, vigor, concentration, and discernment of truth, expert in knowledge and action, aware, slough off this mass of misery.

17. Engineers conduct water, fletchers make arrows true, carpenters straighten wood, the well disciplined train themselves.

XI. Old Age

THIS CHAPTER OFFERS SOME SOBERING CON-
templations of the passage of time, the transitoriness of things, the brevity of youth, and
the approach of old age. Such reflections,
which are to be found in many traditions, do
not represent a philosophy of pessimism, as
some outside observers are inclined to believe, but are exercises dedicated to everyday
sobriety and will. Contemplation of old age is
to be used, above all, to stimulate the individual to take steps to avoid ending up by meet-
ing death without work, passing away
without having really lived.

1. What mirth is there, what joy, while
    constantly burning?

Shrouded in darkness, why not seek a light?

2. See this image, created by mind, a mass of wounds, diseased, pensive, impermanent, and unstable.

3. This material form is decayed, a nest of disease, frail. This putrid body is destroyed, for life ends in death.

4. What attachment is there when one has seen these white bones as like gourds discarded in autumn?

5. The bones are made a citadel, plastered with flesh and blood, in which lie old age and death, pride and contempt.

6. The splendid chariots of kings wear out; so does the body age. Thus do good people teach each other.

Aphorisms 2 through 6 refer to a basic meditation practice. "This image" refers to the body, which is described as a "mass of wounds" in this perspective in view of its normal "oozing" of secretions and waste products. Contemplation of the body as impure, in need of constant cleaning and maintenance, is one of the elementary exercises of the Lesser Journey, not a doctrine of morbidity. In the Greater Journey, contemplation of the body as impure dissolves into contemplation of the body as spacelike.

---

7. A person who has learned little ages like an ox;
   his flesh increases, but not his insight.
8. I have gone through many repeated beginnings
   seeking without finding the maker of this house;
   it is miserable to start over again and again.
9. You have been seen, maker of the house; you will
   not rebuild again. Your framing is all broken,
   your ridgepole destroyed. The mind set on detachment from created things has attained
   extinction of craving.

The "maker of this house" here refers to the individual men-
tality, the myth and illusion maker that sees the body as the
self or treats it like a possession or attribute rather than a
loan. "You will not rebuild again" means that when you have
seen the source of illusion, you do not deceive yourself anymore
with images of false self-importance.

---

10. Those who have not practiced chastity, those who
    have not acquired wealth in youth, ruminate like
    old herons on a little lake without fish.
11. Those who have not practiced chastity, those who
    have not acquired wealth in youth, lie like worn-
    out bows, moaning over the past.

Acquiring wealth in youth refers to richness of character. It
also refers literally to material wealth, whereby one may avoid
being a burden on others, thus making for a less anxious life
and less remorseful passing.

XII. The *Self*

THIS CHAPTER OUTLINES THE CONSCIOUSNESS of the responsible individual, one who is fully aware of the consequences of action and thus is intelligently self-controlled. The need to master oneself before helping others, usually not expected or emphasized in altruistic teachings as ordinarily known or conceived, is introduced here. Unless the compassionate individual is already independent of personal needs by virtue of self-work, compassion degenerates into ineffective sentimentality. This may be seen on every level of human endeavor, from local interactions to international relations.

1. One who knows self is dear will keep it well guarded; the wise one keeps a vigil a third of the night.

It has often been imagined that Buddhism denies self and preaches self-abnegation as the highest ideal. A writer claiming to be an adept at inner and outer yoga even claims that Buddhism is inherently authoritarian and therefore intrinsically abusive because it regards selflessness as the summum bonum. While there may be unscrupulous people who use this idea to control, suppress, or bully others, that is not Buddhism but an aberrant abuse of a misconstrued idea. The seventeenth-century Zen master Suzuki Shosan wrote, "Stand up and be responsible for yourself. . . . Beware of your mind, and take responsibility for yourself." In the same vein, he also wrote, "Be aware of yourself and know yourself. . . . If you don't know yourself, you cannot know anything else."

---

2. One should establish oneself in rectitude first, then one may instruct others; the wise will remain unstained.
3. If one would make oneself as one teaches others to be, one should master self-control, for the self is truly hard to tame.

Classical Zen Buddhists were particularly adamant about the need to be enlightened oneself before trying to teach others. People today seem to think teacherhood is a position.

4. Self is master of self; who else would be the master? With a self well under control, one gains a master hard to find.

The incompatibility of authoritarianism with authentic Buddhism is starkly revealed here. The idea that Buddhism is authoritarian (held even by some followers, especially in the West) is based on false models of Buddhism.

5. The evil done by oneself, born of oneself, produced by oneself, crushes the unintelligent like a diamond does a gemstone.
6. One whose perpetual bad conduct spreads over him as a parasitical vine does a tree makes himself as his enemy wishes him to be.

"Makes himself as his enemy wishes him to be"—people weak in conscience or strong in aggressiveness may find it easier to master themselves by thinking in terms of thwarting the wishes of ill-wishers. Though roundabout, this way of thinking is accurate and effective.

7. It is easy to do what is bad and harmful to oneself; what is beneficial and good is supremely hard to do.

The essential contrast here is between the ease of indulgence and the difficulty of self-mastery.

8. Whoever rejects the teaching of the worthy and noble who live the truth, an imbecile fixated on wrong opinion, produces self-destructive results, like the cane that dies on fruiting.

Hence the danger of accepting secondhand opinions about what a teaching says and means.

9. It is by oneself that evil is done, by oneself that one is afflicted. It is by oneself that evil is not done, by oneself that one is purified. Purity and impurity are individual matters; no one purifies another.

People in a hurry to "find a teacher" to solve their problems for them could do well to digest these lines. To go to a teacher unprepared is to importune a real teacher and to empower a false teacher; what good does it do in either case?

10. Do not neglect your own need for another's, no matter how great; having discerned your own need, do what is really useful.

*The point of this passage is not that you should not help others, but that you **cannot** help others in a real sense, even if you try, unless and until you have first developed your own understanding and capacity to a sufficient degree. Lending a hand just to feel like you are doing some good is really selfish indulgence, not altruistic action. The superficial who are inclined to confuse activism with action are often revealed by their reaction to statements such as this one here in the* **Dhammapada.**

XIII. The World

THIS CHAPTER DEPICTS HAPPINESS IN THIS world and beyond the world. These two kinds of happiness are not seen as contraries, but as a single continuity of spiritual evolution resulting from self-mastery.

1. Do not practice base ways, do not dwell in heedlessness. Do not act on false views, do not increase worldliness.
2. Arise, do not be negligent; practice the principle of good conduct. One who acts on truth is happy in this world and beyond.

3. Practice the principle of good conduct, not evil conduct. One who acts on truth is happy in this world and beyond.

From the perspective illustrated by these first three aphorisms, worldliness and happiness in the world are not the same thing. Even in the Lesser Journey, a follower of Buddhism strives positively and constructively for true happiness in the world without worldliness. The observation is that worldliness, which here means being steeped in worldly views, does not produce happiness but the opposite, because lack of fluidity in handling a transient world ultimately leads to disappointment and sorrow. Disappointment and sorrow are the opposite of Buddhism; they are the objects of observation that Buddhism cuts through by means of perfect insight.

4. Whoever looks upon this world as a bubble, as a mirage, is not seen by the King of Death.

This method of contemplation has been confused with an article of dogma by literal-minded scholars. The great Japanese Zen master Musō Soseki explains that the contemplative method described here is not ultimate, but a method of breaking through fixation on views of the world. This needs to be said, because fixation on the view of the world as a mirage is also an illusion with undesirable consequences. In the **Avatamsaka-sutra,** *there are extensive descriptions of uses of such exercises for attainment and realization of transcendental tolerance in the chapter called* **The Ten Acceptances.**

5. Come, look at this world, like a painted royal chariot; fools sink in it, the knowing have no attachment to it.

"Like a painted royal chariot" means that it may have a splendid appearance but will eventually break down and fall apart. This colorful image is simply a way of practicing recollection of transitoriness.

---

6. One who was formerly negligent, then later becomes vigilant, lights up the world like an unclouded moon.
7. One who uses goodness to cover the evil he has done lights up the world like an unclouded moon.
8. This world is blind; few can see here. Few go to heaven, like birds escaped from a net.
9. Swans travel the path of the sun, magical powers travel through space; the wise are led out of the world, having conquered all bedevilments.

The path of liberation is not like a worldly career that rises and sets like the sun, nor yet like the career of the shaman, who is equally bound, albeit to a different order of interpretation of reality; the path of liberation leads beyond all bondage, ordinary or supernatural. This is an immutable criterion of Buddhist enlightenment.

---

10. One who violates a principle, tells lies, and rejects the world beyond, will refrain from no evil.
11. The avaricious do not go to heaven, the foolish do not extol charity. The wise one, however, rejoicing in charity, becomes thereby happy in the beyond.
12. Better than sole dominion over the earth, or even going to heaven; better than lordship over all worlds is the fruit of entering the stream.

"Entering the stream" is a technical term for an initial stage of Buddhist realization: It is perhaps most simply defined as putting an end to delusion by views and opinions.

XIV. The Enlightened

THIS CHAPTER PRESENTS CAPSULES OF TRADI-
tional summaries of basic teachings of
Buddha—the liberty of the enlightened, the
four noble truths, the noble eightfold path,
the peace and freedom of nirvana.

1. By what track can you lead the trackless
   one, the enlightened one, with infinite
   perception, the one whose victory is
   not overturned, whose victory none in
   the world can approach?
2. By what track can you lead the trackless
   one, the enlightened one, with infinite
   perception, whom no ensnaring craving
   can carry away?

A classical Zen proverb says, "An elephant does not walk a rabbit's path; great enlightenment does not retain a teacher."

3. Even the gods wish to be as the wise ones devoted to meditation, delighting in the calm of detachment, perfectly awakened, imbued with mindfulness.
4. It is hard to get to be human; the life of mortals is hard. Teaching of truth is hardly ever heard; Buddhas hardly ever appear.

Union of Difference and Sameness, *one of the early Chinese Zen classics, begins and ends with lines reminiscent of this aphorism, which lines some commentators say bear the gist of the whole message: "The mind of Buddha is communicated inwardly, East or West. . . . Don't waste time!"*

5. Not to do any evils, to accomplish good, to purify one's own mind—this is the teaching of the enlightened.

The outstanding Japanese Zen master Dogen wrote a whole essay, **Do Not Do Anything Evil,** *on nothing but the inner and outer meanings of this famous saying.*

6. Patient forbearance is the supreme austerity; nirvana is called by the Buddha supreme. One who

harms others is not a renunciant; one who causes
harm to others is not an ascetic.

Gautama Buddha redefined renunciation and asceticism as
abstention from what is harmful, rather than escapism and
avoidance of the world.

---

7. Not insulting, not injuring, self-discipline, moderation in consumption, solitude, exertion in
   mental concentration—this is the teaching of the
   Buddhas.

Solitude means being aloof from the influences of society. It
may be practiced alone or in company, just as emotional
dependency can be practiced alone or in company. One who is
physically alone yet still under the influence of other people is
not solitary. One who abandons the world in favor of isolation
is not solitary either, because the world is still a companion by
virtue of ongoing relation, even though that relation be one of
rejection.

Pang Yun, a freethinking scholar of eighth-century China,
once asked a great Zen master, "Who is the one that does not
keep company with myriad things?" The master said, "I'll tell
you when you swallow the water of the West River in one gulp."

Pang Yun attained awakening at these words. Embracing
the totality of being is a direct method of attaining the
supreme solitude without losing sight of the plight of the
world.

8. There is no satisfaction of desires, even by a
   shower of money. One is wise to know that desires are painful, bringing little enjoyment.

Desires are painful in the sense that a state of permanent sen-
sual gratification is biologically impossible, and therefore it is
painful to exaggerate gratification of desires into an end in
itself. The Buddha recommends "eating with perfect knowl-
edge" of the function of desire as an instinctively programmed
mechanism for activating the body, not the reason for life itself.

One exercise that can be useful to those who may not see
things this way is to make a detailed inventory of their own
lives and experiences, taking care to try to distinguish subjec-
tively related experiences of anticipation, hope, worry, fear,
anxiety, disappointment, and so on, from the actual or sup-
posed experience of a specific gratification. Try to assess the
relative amount of concern, planning, effort, and so on, associ-
ated with specific satisfactions. Also be sure to distinguish the
primary experience, the aftertaste, and the memory. After
having done this, you may at least discover what you might
reasonably think worthwhile or otherwise, and why, if that
matters to you in your thought and behavior. This exercise can
therefore be just as useful for cultivating constructive under-
standing as it is for cultivating understanding that is destruc-
tive of clinging obsession.

---

9. Finding no delight even in celestial pleasures, the
   rightly awakened disciple delights in the destruction of craving.

The point of this passage is that Buddhist meditation is not practiced for the purpose of enjoying altered states of consciousness (represented by "celestial pleasures").

10–11. People compelled by fear go to many a refuge—mountains, forests, resorts, trees, and shrines. That is not a safe refuge, that is not the ultimate refuge; one is not freed of all miseries by going to that refuge.

After examining "religion" or "spiritual seeking" from this point of view, one can understand the Buddha's emphasis on independent liberation through perfect insight with even greater clarity.

12–13. But one who takes refuge in the enlightened, the teaching, and the community, sees the four noble truths with accurate insight: misery, the origin of misery, and the overcoming of misery; and the noble eightfold path that leads to cessation of misery.

14. This indeed is a safe refuge; this is the ultimate refuge. Having come to this refuge, one is freed from all misery.

The "community" literally and spiritually refers to those who resort to truth through the teaching expounded by the enlight-

ened. *The meaning of this is not just confessional, devotional, or institutional, but essentially spiritual. This is illustrated in the* **Avatamsaka-sutra***'s book called* **The Meditation of the Enlightening Being Universally Good.** *The* **Mahaparinirvana-sutra** *defines the true community as universal love and objective reality itself.*

The four noble truths are basic facts to which Buddhists resort:

1) *conditioned states are unsatisfactory*
2) *this misery has a cause*
3) *this misery has an end*
4) *there is a way to the end of this misery*

These truths are most colorfully defined and illustrated in the **Avatamsaka-sutra,** *in the book called* **The Four Holy Truths.** *The way to end misery, in this context, refers to the noble eightfold path to nirvana:*

1) *accurate perception*
2) *accurate thinking*
3) *accurate speech*
4) *appropriate action*
5) *appropriate way of making a living*
6) *precise effort*
7) *right recollection*
8) *right concentration*

15. A noble person is hard to find; one is not born
    everywhere. Wherever such a wise one is born,
    that family attains felicity.

*Here Buddha reverses Hindu Brahminism: In Buddhism,
birth does not define nobility, nobility defines birth.*

16. Felicitous is the emergence of the enlightened, fe-
    licitous is the teaching of truth. Felicitous is
    harmony in the community, felicitous the auster-
    ity of those in harmony.

17–18. None can measure the virtue of one who is mak-
    ing offerings to one worthy of offering, whether a
    Buddha or a disciple, to one who has gone be-
    yond false rationalizations and crossed over
    sorrow and grief; none can measure the virtue of
    one making offerings to such as have attained nir-
    vana and are free from all fear.

*The idea behind this is not to create an artificial class of
impudent beggars in expensive finery, but to encourage societies to encourage what is best in human nature and character.*

XV. Happiness

THIS CHAPTER REPRESENTS AN IMAGE OF transcendental happiness through inner release, a state of tranquillity free from hatred, free from restlessness, and free from fear. The sublime happiness described herein is presented as the state of the real human being, "wise, insightful, learned, enduring, dutiful, noble."

1. Let us live most happily, free from hatred in the midst of the hateful; let us remain free from hatred in the midst of people who hate.
2. Let us live most happily, free from disease in the midst of the diseased; let us remain free from disease in the midst of diseased people.

3. Let us live most happily, free from restlessness in the midst of the restless; let us remain free from restlessness in the midst of restlessness.

These first three aphorisms underscore the message that inner peace is not won by trying to reject the world, but by living in its midst without being the slave of greed, hatred, and folly.

4. Let us live most happily, possessing nothing; let us feed on joy, like the radiant gods.

Feeding on joy means savoring the taste of abstract contemplation instead of savoring thoughts of ambition and acquisition.

5. Victory breeds hatred; the defeated sleeps in misery. One who has calmed down sleeps in comfort, having given up victory and defeat.

The **Tao Te Ching** *says, "Extreme fondness means great expense, and abundant possessions mean much loss. If you know when you have enough, you will not be disgraced. If you know when to stop, you will not be endangered. It is possible thereby to live long."*

6. There is no fire like passion, no bad luck like hatred. There is no misery like physical existence, no happiness higher than tranquillity.

The Tao Te Ching says, "The reason that we have so much trouble is that we have bodies." This can also be read, "The reason that we have so much trouble is that we have selves." A basic Buddhist exercise is to recollect such statements in times of both health and sickness, in both good and bad moods, to observe the differences in your own feelings and reactions in response to reminders of vulnerability and mortality.

7. Hunger is the worst illness, conditioned states are the worst miseries. When you know this as it is, nirvana is the highest happiness.

Contentment is described as a garment that never wears out.

8. Health is the best acquisition, satisfaction is the best wealth. Trust is the best relation, nirvana is the best pleasure.
9. Having imbibed the flavor of solitude and the flavor of tranquillity, one becomes free from fear and free from evil, drinking the juice of delight in truth.
10. The sight of the noble is good, association with them is always happy. One who never sees fools will be happy forever.
11. One who walks with fools will sorrow a long way; for the company of fools is miserable, as that of an enemy, always.

12. Wise, insightful, learned, enduring, dutiful, noble—follow one who is like this, a real human being, truly intelligent, as the moon follows the path of the stars.

Spiritual seekers would be less confused about teachers and their authenticity if they would look beyond appearances to see real qualities. Under these conditions, and providing one knows one's own biases well enough to keep them at bay, it is not that hard to distinguish reality and falsehood in people.

XVI. Pleasure

THIS CHAPTER FOCUSES ON THE SIMPLE FACT
that obsessive pursuit of pleasure causes
pain. It causes pain to the obsessive pleasure
seeker as well as to those who are deprived
and abused by the selfish and ambitious behavior resulting from this obsession. A necessary step to inner peace and a happy life,
therefore, is understanding the nature and
consequences of bondage to compulsive acquisitiveness.

1. Involved in distraction, not engaging in
   unifying effort, one who gives up what
   is necessary through obsession with
   what is pleasing will envy one who de-
   votes himself to unification.

2. Never cleave to what is pleasing or what is displeasing; not seeing what is pleasant is painful, and so is seeing what is unpleasant.

3. So do not take a liking to anything, for loss of what is liked is bad. There are no fetters for those who have no likes or dislikes.

4. Sorrow arises from what is dear, fear arises from what is dear. For someone free from liking, there is no sorrow; how could there be fear?

5. Sorrow arises from affection, fear arises from affection. For someone free from affection, there is no sorrow; how could there be fear?

6. Sorrow arises from enjoyment, fear arises from enjoyment. For someone free from enjoyment, there is no sorrow; how could there be fear?

7. Sorrow arises from desire, fear arises from desire. For someone free from desire, there is no sorrow; how could there be grief?

8. Sorrow arises from craving, fear arises from craving. For someone free from craving, there is no sorrow; how could there be fear?

The underlying logic of the statements in 4 to 8 is outlined in aphorisms 2 and 3 preceding.

9. Perfected in conduct and vision, standing on truth, veracious in speech, minding one's own business—such a one the world holds dear.

10. One who aspires to the ineffable, who is pervaded

with consciousness, and whose mind is unattached to desires, is called one who swims against
the stream.

In this context, to "swim against the stream" means to be
immune to the forces of opinion and outmoded habit that
ordinarily prevent people from examining their own nature
and fate from any other vantage point.

11–12. When a person long absent from home re-
turns safely from afar, relatives, friends, and
well-wishers rejoice at his return. In the same
way, when one who has done good is gone
from this world to the beyond, his good deeds
receive him, like relatives receiving a return-
ing loved one.

In the vocabulary of Islam, similarly, one is said to "send
onward" or "forward" the results of one's actions, to be experi-
enced in the recapitulation at the end of this life.

XVII. Anger

THIS CHAPTER DWELLS ON THE ADVANTAGES of freedom from anger and ill will. Certain aphorisms also provide practical insight on how to overcome these irritations in oneself, and even in others, by transformation of outlook and habit.

1. Abandon anger, give up pride; overcome all attachment. No miseries befall one who does not cling to name and form.

Name and form mean ideas and objects in general. Clinging to ideas and objects as real or sacred in themselves, rather than as functional or dysfunctional in their place, is a form of idolatry.

2. One who controls occurring anger as one would a chariot gone off the track, that one I call a charioteer; other people just hold the reins.
3. Overcome anger by nonanger, overcome evil by good. Overcome the miser by giving, overcome the liar by truth.

Buddhist nonviolence is not limited to passive resistance, but also includes active transmutation.

---

4. Speak the truth, do not become angered, and give when asked, even be it a little. By these three conditions one goes to the presence of the gods.
5. Sages who do no harm, who are always in control of the body, go to an everlasting abode, where they will not sorrow.
6. In those who are ever-wakeful, who study day and night, devoted to nirvana, compulsions come to an end.
7. It is an old saying, not a new one: "They disparage one who remains silent, they disparage one who talks a lot, and they even disparage one who speaks in moderation." There is no one in the world who is not disparaged.
8. There has never been, never will be, and is not now anyone who is absolutely disparaged or absolutely praised.

Aphorisms 7 and 8 demonstrate a contemplation to free the individual from what we now call peer pressure. You cannot please everyone, no matter what you do, so watch yourself, watch out for yourself, and seek the truth itself.

9–10. Who is capable of praising one like a coin of finest gold, one whom the knowing praise after finding him impeccable, controlled, intelligent, insightful, ethical, and composed day in and day out? Even the gods praise such a one, even the Creator.

The name of the last prophet of the Abrahamic tradition, who embodied these qualities, literally means Praised One. A similar description is given in a hymn of the Torah.

11. Guard against physical agitation, be restrained in physical action. Give up misconduct of the body, practice good conduct with the body.

12. Guard against irritation in speech, be restrained in speech. Give up misconduct in speech, practice good conduct in speaking.

13. Guard against mental irritation, be restrained in mind. Give up misconduct of mind, practice good conduct in mind.

14. The wise who control body, speech, and mind are indeed the consummately controlled.

Body, speech, and mind are called the Three Mysteries in Esoteric Tantric Buddhism, wherein the seeker at a certain stage envisions the direct identification, or elemental continuity, of the Three Mysteries in oneself and the Three Mysteries of Buddha as cosmic realities.

XVIII. Impurity

THIS CHAPTER DESCRIBES AND DEFINES THE sort of impurities that need to be cleared away before inner peace is realized, and introduces certain meditations to assist the process. By awareness of impurity, it is held, the vigilance necessary for liberation can be developed naturally.

1. You are now like a withered leaf; the very heralds of Death have come near to you. You stand at the door of departure, but you have no provisions for the journey.
2. Make an island for yourself, get right to work; become wise. When you are purged of impurity and free of mental taint, you will reach the noble state of heaven.

3. You have now come to the end of your life; you have arrived in the presence of Death. There is no resting place for you on the way, and you have no provisions for the journey.

For practical purposes, it is critical to remember that aphorisms like these represent contemplative exercises, not philosophical dogma.

---

4. Make an island for yourself, get right to work; become wise. When you are purged of impurity and free of taint, you will not enter into birth and old age anymore.
5. Let the intelligent one get rid of the impurity of the self gradually, little by little, moment to moment, as a metalworker removes impurity from silver.
6. Just as rust eats away the iron from which it is produced, so do their own deeds lead the overindulgent into a miserable state.
7. Nonrecitation is impurity for an incantation, inactivity is impurity for a house, indolence is impurity of character, negligence is impurity in a guardian.
8. Misconduct is impurity in a woman, stinginess is impurity in a donor. Evil ways are impurities in this world and the beyond.

9. Even more impure than those impurities is ignorance, the supreme impurity. Casting this
impurity away, be undefiled.

---

*Buddhism considers ignorance to be the root of all evil; thus it
is the supreme impurity.*

---

10. Life is easy to live for the shameless, for the impudent, for the spoiler, for the braggart, for the
reckless, for the impure.
11. But life is hard to live for the modest always seeking purity, for the independent, for the
circumspect, for the seer who lives in purity.

---

*The difficulty and ease spoken of here in aphorisms 10 and 11
often concern the agreement or opposition of the surrounding
society more than the actual individual energetic cost of the
actions involved.*

12–13. Whoever destroys life, speaks untruth, takes what
is not given, resorts to another's wife, or gives
himself up to liquor, digs out his own root right
here in this world.
14. Know this, O humankind: Evil ways go un-
checked; do not let greed and wrongdoing stir up
long-term misery for you.

We can only control our own actions; just as we cannot neces-sarily protect others from the consequences of their own deeds, we cannot fairly expect others to rescue us from the conse-quences of our own deeds, when we have exercised our right or freedom to choose our way.

15–16. People give according to belief or faith; so whoever is depressed about the food and drink of
another never attains concentration, either by day
or by night. But when this is cut off, extirpated
by the root, then one attains concentration by day
and by night.

Institutionalized formats that allow competitiveness to breed always end up failing to actualize living Buddhism, regardless of how they may appear to the outward eye, because there is an inherent "leak" or "drain" preventing concentration on truth from building up.

17. There is no fire like passion, no captor like hatred, no snare like delusion, no torrent like
craving.

18. It is easy to see the fault of others, hard to see
one's own. One sifts the faults of others like
chaff, but covers up one's own, as a crafty cheater
covers up a losing throw.

19. In one who watches out for the faults of others, always ready to blame, compulsions increase; such a
one is far from extinction of compulsion.

20. There is no road in the sky, there is no asceticism in externals; mankind delights in falsehood, those who realize suchness are free from falsehood.

21. There is no road in the sky, there is no asceticism in externals; there is no permanence in conditioned things, there is no vacillation in Buddhas.

———————————

These aphorisms explain why the way of the enlightened is "trackless" and cannot be reduced to fixed dogma and ritual performance. ———————————

XIX. The Righteous

THIS CHAPTER CONTRASTS DEFINITIONS OF worth based on superficial appearances and conventional performances with definitions of worth based on the inner realities of being and the ennoblement of character.

1. One who forces his way to gain is not righteous; one is sagacious when one has determined both what is beneficial and what is not.
2. One who guides others without force, righteously and equitably, is called a guardian of the teaching, wise and just.

This aphorism illustrates essential aspects of the incompatibility of authoritarianism with authentically effective Buddhist education.

3. One is not wise just because one talks a lot; one who is calm, free from hostility, and without fear, is said to be sagacious.

4. One is not a bearer of the teaching just because one talks a lot; one who sees the teaching bodily, even though little learned, one who does not neglect the teaching, is indeed a bearer of the teaching.

5. One is not an elder because one's hair has gone gray; though ripe of age, it may be said one has grown old in vain.

6. One in whom are truth, justice, nonviolence, restraint, and control is indeed purged of impurity, wise; *then* one is called an elder.

7. Not merely by talking, nor by beauty of appearance, does an envious, avaricious cheat become fair.

8. The one from whom that is extirpated, totally uprooted, the wise one freed from corruption, is the one who is called fair.

9. One who is undisciplined and speaks untruth is not an ascetic by virtue of having a shaven head; how can one full of desire and acquisitiveness be an ascetic?

10. But one who stills all evils, great and small, is called an ascetic, because of having stilled all evils.

11. One is not a mendicant just because of begging from others. One is a mendicant when one has accepted the whole truth, not until then.

12. One who is chaste, having transcended both good and evil, and who acts with consideration in the world, that one is called a mendicant.

13–14. One who is deluded and ignorant does not become a sage by silence; but the sage is the wise one who, holding the scale, takes to that which is best.

15. One who harms living beings is not ennobled; one who is harmless to all living beings is called noble.

16–17. Not merely by rules of conduct and religious observances, nor by much learning either, nor even by attainment of concentration, nor by sleeping alone, do I reach the happiness of freedom, to which no worldlings attain. If you have not put an end to compulsions, nurse your faith.

Aphorisms 3 through 17 reiterate in different ways the principle that one should look beyond superficial appearances and labels to see real inner qualities. They also demonstrate that the ritual externals and performances of monasteries are not spiritually essential to Buddhist practice.

XX. The Path

THIS CHAPTER OUTLINES THE WAY TO PURI-
fication of mind and attainment of inner
peace taught by Buddha. Special emphasis is
placed on the idea that the Buddha only
shows the way, and that the actual application
is an individual choice and responsibility that
can be taken up only by free will. The path is
not fostered by coercive authoritarian measures, but by firsthand recognition of the
truths underlying the path.

1. The eightfold is the best of paths; the
   four statements are the best of truths.
   Dispassion is the best of principles;
   seers are the best of humans.

For the eightfold path and four truths, see notes above on XIV.10–14.

2. This is the path; there is no other conducive to
   purification of vision. You should follow this one,
   for it throws off the Killer.

The Killer refers to delusion or "bedevilment," which kills the life of wisdom.

3. Following this path, you will put an end to your
   misery. I declared the path after having understood how to relieve pain.
4. You must make the effort; the Buddhas just tell
   you how. The contemplatives who follow the path
   are free from the bonds of the Killer.

The relationship between a guide and a seeker is not one of emotional, intellectual, or institutional dependency; no amount of help can do for us what we need to do for ourselves.

5. When one sees by insight that all conditioned
   states are transitory, one then wearies of misery;
   this is the path to purity.
6. When one sees by insight that all conditioned
   states are miserable, one then wearies of misery;
   this is the path to purity.

In common parlance among Westerners, the first truth has often been exaggerated into the overstatement that life is suffering. The critical issue is bondage to conditioned states, and liberation from this bondage. Far from being pessimistic, as has so often been said in respect to overstatement of the first truth, Buddhism is the epitome of optimism, believing that humanity can rise, both individually and collectively, above its folly, greed, and aggression.

7. When one sees by insight that all things are self-
    less, then one wearies of misery; this is the path
    to purity.

It is noteworthy that the **Dhammapada** *makes no direct reference to the selflessness of persons, speaking only of the selflessness of things. This is in accord with the view of the Greater
Journey, in which the selflessness of persons is realized as a
positive fact of unlimited potential based on the selflessness of
all phenomena. In Buddhist yoga, the inner aspect of the
teaching, the real characteristic of things, is referred to as the
selflessness of things in* **suchness.**

8. The idler who does not arise when it is time to
    arise, who is full of sloth though young and
    strong, who is lazy and weak in thought and
    mind, does not find the path to insight.

Those who wish to transcend the world by thoughtless medita-
tion may reach any degree of thoughtlessness, but they will not
reach completion that way. They do not even reach insight, as
this aphorism explains. Most of all, they do not see through
their own thoughtlessness. These are the people who get
caught by pretentious gurus; some of them become pretentious
gurus themselves.

9. Always careful in speech and restrained in mind,
   one should not do wrong with the body. One
   should purify these three ways of action, and attain the path taught by the seers.
10. Wisdom arises through effort, wisdom disappears
    through lack of effort; knowing this twofold path
    of growth and decline, one should arrange oneself
    such that wisdom increases.

"One should arrange oneself such that wisdom increases." This
is one of the simplest yet most sophisticated exercises; how to
arrange the items of one's life, including one's thoughts and
feelings, conversations and activities, such that they yield the
maximum insight and understanding of life itself and
the minimum unnecessary distraction and vexation. Among
the problems people seem to experience in the process of self-
renewal is to imagine they need to remove or replace what they
only need rearrange, and imagine they need only rearrange
what they need to remove or replace.

11. Cut down the forest, not the tree; danger comes from the forest. Having cut down the forest and craving as well, you will attain nirvana.

According to the **Mahaparinirvana-sutra,** *the tree represents the body, the forest is the thicket of thoughts. The classical Zen master Baizhang said, "The forest symbolizes mind, the tree symbolizes the body. Fear is aroused because of talk about the forest, so it is said, 'Chop down the forest, not the tree.'" This underscores the point that Buddhist abstinence and renunciation do not mean torturing the body but rather clearing the mind.*

---

12. As long as a man's desire for women, however little, is not cut through, so long is his mind attached, like a suckling calf to its mother.

Superficial interpreters believe this means it is impossible for enlightened people to share loving feelings and sensual enjoyment as well as they can share sorrow and pain. Paradoxically, even those who adopt this interpretation often seem to disbelieve in detachment, with the result that there are married monks fathering children supported by celibate workers, and lay people dogmatically worrying about repressing or indulging their sensuality instead of transforming their experience of it.

---

13. Uproot self-love, as you would an autumn lily by hand; cherish the path to peace, to nirvana taught by the Felicitous One.

The Felicitous One (Sugata, Gone to Felicity) is one of the standard descriptive epithets of a Buddha.

14. "I will live here during the rainy season, here in
     winter and summer"—so thinks the fool, un-
     aware of the obstacle.

The classical Zen master Yunmen said, "Don't waste time traveling through the countryside, spending a winter here and a summer there, enjoying the scenery, whatever captivates you, casting in your lot wherever there are a lot of meals provided. Ouch! Ouch! In planning for that one sack of rice, you have lost half a year's provisions! If you go on 'pilgrimage' like this, what benefit will there be?"

15. A man whose mind is obsessed with children and
     chattels is carried away by death like a sleeping
     village by a flood.
16. Children are no protection, nor father, nor yet
     kin; there is no refuge in relatives, for one over-
     taken by death.
17. Realizing the meaning of this, the wise one
     guarded in conduct should quickly clear the path
     that goes to nirvana.

Aphorisms 15 to 17 do not mean we should abandon our children and desert our families and homes, but that we should abandon our own subjective obsessions about them and deal with people and things objectively, above all not expecting their love and affection to absolve us of our own responsibilities, and realizing our own love and affection for them does not remove the responsibility of their own consciousness and their own journey from the shoulders of their own experience. People may help each other, but they cannot live each other's lives for them. The wandering Pure Land Buddhist saint Ippen said, "There are three types of person who practice remembrance of Buddha. Those of the highest faculties attain Rebirth even while being married householders with children by not being obsessive. Those of middling faculties may give up spouses and children, but still have places to live, food, and clothing; yet by not being obsessive, they do attain Rebirth. Those of lowest faculties attain Rebirth by relinquishing everything. I act as I do because I am of the lowest faculties, and am sure I would cling to things at the moment of death and thus fail to be Reborn if I did not give up everything." When he was challenged by someone who pointed out that his explanation seemed to differ from that of a certain scripture, the saint explained, "All Buddhist teachings deal with states of mind, not external appearances. Leaving home and giving up ambitions mentally, not sticking obsessively to anything, is considered characteristic of the higher sort."

XXI. Miscellany

AS THE TITLE INDICATES, THIS CHAPTER DEALS with a number of topics. The aphorisms collected here generally concern seeing beyond limited temporary pleasures to ultimate happiness, directing thought to the causes of bondage and freedom, and awakening the mind to reality.

1. If by giving up limited pleasures one sees far-reaching happiness, the wise one leaves aside limited pleasures, looking to far-reaching happiness.
2. One who seeks his own pleasure by means that inflict suffering on others, tangled up in enmity, is not freed from hatred.

The principles stated in aphorisms 1 and 2 are also successfully applied in the fields of business and diplomacy.

3. If they neglect what should be done, and do what should not be done, compulsions increase in the arrogant and careless.

4. But in the mindful and discerning whose consciousness is alert and always focused on the body, who do not attend to what is not to be done, persevering in what should be done, compulsions come to an end.

Focus on the body has three stages. In the Lesser Journey, the focus is on transitoriness, mortality, and the need for constant cleaning and maintenance. In the Greater Journey, the focus is on spacelike ethereality. In the Tantra, or Fundamental Continuity, focus is on purity.

5. Killing mother and father, and two warrior kings, killing a kingdom with all its subjects, the priestly one goes untroubled.

Mother and father stand for greed and conceit. The two warrior kings are grasping and rejecting. The kingdom with all its subjects is the totality of the individual's experience of life in the domain of conditioned existence.

6. Killing mother and father, and two learned kings,
   killing five eminent men, the priestly one goes
   untroubled.

---

*The two learned kings are notions of eternalism and nihilism.
The five eminent men are passion, rage, stupefaction, excita-
tion followed by regret, and doubt.*

---

7. Those who hear Gautama are always wide-awake,
   their thought on the enlightened one day and
   night.
8. Those who hear Gautama are always wide-awake,
   their thought on the teaching day and night.
9. Those who hear Gautama are always wide-awake,
   their thought on the community day and night.
10. Those who hear Gautama are always wide-awake,
    their thought on the body day and night.
11. Those who hear Gautama are always wide-awake,
    their thought on harmlessness day and night.
12. Those who hear Gautama are always wide-awake,
    their thought on cultivation day and night.

---

*"Those who hear Gautama" means those who follow Gautama
Buddha's teaching, not worshipers of Buddha as a "Lord."*

---

13. Homes are miserable; hard to leave, hard to en-
    joy, hard to live in. Living with the uncongenial is

miserable, the vagrant is beset by misery. So let
no one become a vagrant, let no one be dogged
by misery.

---

*"Homes" symbolize psychological holdings acquired through
habit and conditioning.*

14. The faithful one perfect in conduct, to whom are
    granted fame and prosperity, is honored in every
    place.
15. Good people shine from afar, like the Snowy
    Mountains; those who are no good are not seen
    here, like arrows shot in the night.
16. Sitting alone, sleeping alone, acting alone, let the
    diligent one enjoy the forest, taming the self
    alone.

XXII. Hell

THIS CHAPTER ASSEMBLES APHORISMS DEAL-
ing specifically with the nature of habitual
attitudes and behaviors that lead to the worst
possible results. These roads to hell, furthermore, are not only mundane profanities but
also include superficial and hypocritical religious vocations and observances. Extreme
asceticism or mortification, shunning what
need not be avoided, and similar prejudices
of judgment and action are specially presented as warnings to those inclined to zealo-
try in the name of spirituality.

1. One who speaks untruth goes to hell, as
   does one who claims not to have done
   what he has in fact done. Both become

equal after death, people of base deeds in the hereafter.

2. Many who wear the saffron robe are evil and unrestrained. Evildoers go to hell by their evil deeds.

3. It is better for an unethical and unrestrained person to swallow a red-hot iron ball than to consume food obtained from the people.

The idea that the monks were actually the moral or spiritual elite of Buddhism does not square with what we know of actual history, as evidenced, for example, in aphorisms like 2 and 3. The point of this observation is not to demean real monks, but to illustrate the fallacy of a contemporary tendency among some Western Buddhists to demean and even abandon the scriptural teachings themselves because of the failures of some of those persons and groups who claim to represent a select community upholding the teachings. The irony, and the fallacy, of this tendency is that the very same Western groups retain the very same elements that breed corruption, such as authoritarian and competitive structures, while thinking they have purged themselves of medieval elements by rejecting the classical teachings. If, in contrast, those who claimed to be teachers and those who claimed to be Buddhist communities were examined in the light of the Dharma, the teaching that is itself considered a permanent Dharmakaya or body of Buddha, much less confusion about authority and authenticity of people or practices would prevail among those attempting to view and apply Buddhism from the point of view of an imitative quasi-Oriental devotional cult. An unfortunate complica-

tion is the use of mistranslated and misinterpreted materials by inauthentic teachers, making it more difficult to see the otherwise obvious contradictions. Gautama Buddha himself recommended that people study reality carefully and thoughtfully.

4. A heedless man who courts another's wife gets into four states: degradation, inability to sleep peacefully, blame, and hell.
5. Degradation, an evil way of life, the little enjoyment of the fearful by the fearful, and the heavy penalty decreed by the ruler: for these reasons, a man should not court another's wife.
6. Just as a blade of grass wrongly grasped cuts into the hand, asceticism wrongly held to drags one into hell.

Far from reducing selfishness, the asceticism of the selfish increases egocentrism and conceit. The **I Ching** *says, "Regulation is successful, but painful regulation is not to be held to."*

7. An act carelessly performed, a religious observance adulterated with worldly passion, chastity practiced with hesitation—these have no great results.

These aphorisms invite careful reflection.

8. If something is to be done, do it with vigor. A
   careless renunciant scatters more dust.

"A careless renunciant scatters more dust" in the sense that an
escapist causes more trouble by escapism than the original
trouble that was there to begin with.

---

9. Not doing anything is better than doing evil; evil-
   doing causes remorse later on. Better than doing
   just anything is doing something good, a deed
   one will not regret.
10. As a frontier city is guarded inside and out, so
    should you guard your self. Do not let even a
    moment slip by, for those who let the moments
    slip by grieve when they have been consigned to
    hell.
11. They are ashamed of what is not shameful, and
    not ashamed of what is shameful; people who take
    on false views go to an evil state.

Mencius said that the purpose of shame is to enable us to reach
a point where we can be unashamed.

---

12. Seeing danger in what is not dangerous, seeing no
    danger in what is dangerous, people who take on
    false views go to an evil state.

These aphorisms indirectly urge the thinker to examine his or her ideas of what is shameful and/or dangerous, what is to be avoided and what need not be avoided. This is not a superficial exercise in formulation of dogmatic policy or pious hopes, but an exercise in ongoing vigilance and examination of factual patterns.

13. Thinking that what need not be avoided should be shunned, seeing no need to avoid what should be shunned, people who take on false views go to an evil state.

14. Knowing what is to be shunned is to be avoided, knowing what need not be avoided need not be shunned, people who accept right views go to a good state.

XXIII. The Elephant

THIS CHAPTER CENTERS AROUND DIFFERENT associations of the elephant as a symbol of the self. One who has accomplished self-mastery is likened to a tamed elephant, while the unruly self is likened to an elephant in rut. This chapter conveys the mood of the traveler on the path, and emphasizes specific criteria for choosing associates and companions on the way.

1. I will endure abusive words like the elephant in battle endures the arrow shot from the bow; for many people are ill-behaved.

2. They lead a tamed elephant into battle, a king mounts a tamed elephant; the

tamed one is the best of human beings, the one who endures abusive words.

3. Excellent are mules that are tamed, horses of good breed, and the mighty bull elephant; even better is one whose self is tamed.

4. For it is not by these vehicles that one may go to the place of inaccessibility, where the tamed one goes, with self-mastery, by virtue of being tamed.

5. The elephant called Guardian of Treasure is hard to control when in rut. It does not eat any food when bound; the elephant longs for the elephant grove.

6. The fool who becomes a sluggard and a glutton, tossing and turning in sleep, like a fat fodder-fed hog, enters the womb again and again.

To "enter the womb again and again" means to enter into a matrix of dependency again and again by the inertia of subconscious habits.

---

7. This mind used to roam about where it wished, where it wanted, where it pleased; now I will control it judiciously, as the holder of the hook controls an elephant in rut.

8. Take pleasure in vigilance, guard your own mind; extricate yourself from the way to misery, as you would an elephant sunk in the mud.

9. If you find a prudent companion, a wise associate who leads a good life, having overcome all troubles, travel with that one, uplifted and aware.

10. If you do not find a prudent companion, a wise associate leading a good life, then travel alone, like a king abandoning a domain he has conquered, like an elephant roaming the forest.

11. It is better to walk alone; there is no companionship with a fool. Walk alone, like an elephant in the forest, with few desires, doing no evil.

Here in aphorisms 9 through 11 are more guidelines for those who seek teachers and companions.

12. Companionship is pleasant when a need arises; satisfaction is pleasant when it is mutual. Virtue is pleasant at the end of life; pleasant is relinquishment of all misery.

13. Pleasant is motherliness in the world, and fatherliness is pleasant. Pleasant is religiousness in the world, and priestliness is pleasant.

14. Pleasant is morality that lasts to old age; pleasant is faith well-founded. Pleasant is attainment of insight; pleasant is avoidance of evil.

Aphorisms 12 through 14 are not definitions of a dogma of rejection or negation, but of the practice of discerning the relative value of things in their places, considered in the context of the totality of life and death.

XXIV. Craving

THIS CHAPTER RECAPITULATES THE DELUSIVE
and destructive effects of craving, infatua-
tion, and rumination over things, contrasting
their undesirable effects with the freedom
that comes with insight, dispassion, and inner completeness.

1. The craving of a man who acts care-
    lessly grows like a creeping vine. He
    jumps around here and there, like a
    monkey in a forest seeking fruit.
2. Whoever this clinging vulgar craving
    overcomes in the world has sorrows
    that grow like rained-upon grass.

3. Whoever overcomes this clinging vulgar craving in the world, so hard to get over, has sorrows fall away, like drops of water from a lotus.

4. I will tell all of you gathered here something good: Uproot craving entirely, as the seeker of a fragrant root digs out the grass above, so the Killer may not destroy you over and over again, as a torrent destroys reeds.

5. Just as a tree will regrow even if cut, as long as its root has not been destroyed and is firm, so will this misery regrow again and again as long as the tendency to craving is not rooted out.

6. The currents carry away the one who sees wrongly, thoughts fixated on passion, whose thirty-six streams gush toward what is pleasing.

"Thirty-six streams" refer to the total potential of sense experience. There are, in the reckoning of Buddhist psychology, six senses, which also combine with each other to weave the fabric of experience. Hence the matrix of the complexities of our total experience of this world may be referred to as six times sixfold or thirty-six-fold. The "streams" are successions, apparent continuities, of moments of sense experience. It is not that the senses are bad, as explained earlier, but **compulsively following** *sense experience makes one vulnerable to external influences, even external control. That is why liberative nirvana is not destruction or obliteration of sense and perception, but freedom of mind and thought in the very midst of sense and perception.*

---

7. The streams flow everywhere; the creeper, having sprung up, becomes established. When you see that creeper sprout, sever its root by intense insight.

The "creeper" is insidious suggestion, rooted in ignorance and craving, developing into bondage, aggression, and folly. To sever it the moment it sprouts is what the **Tao Te Ching** *refers to as doing what is difficult when it is still easy. This is the purpose of vigilance, so highly recommended by Buddha.*

8. Gushing affections and delights occur to people; attached to comfort, seeking pleasure, such people undergo birth and old age.
9. People compelled by craving crawl like a snared rabbit; bound by a combination of attachments, they undergo suffering again and again, for a long time.
10. People compelled by craving crawl like a snared rabbit; so let the mendicant slough off craving, seeking dispassion for the self.
11. Whoever is freed of craving yet inclined to desire though free of desire runs back to desire; see that very person who, freed, runs back into bondage.

There have evidently always been people who entered monastic life as careerists to make a living. The classical Zen master Linji referred to them as having left one home to enter another, not really transcending mundane attachment.

12. The wise do not say a fetter is strong if it is iron,
    wood, or jute, but infatuation with pearl earrings,
    and desire for sons and wives.

---

*Wealth and status, represented here by ornaments and family,
are not themselves "bad," but the greedy and possessive attitudes people project upon them prevent completion and fulfill-
ment even on the material and social plane, to say nothing of
vitiating the power of any leftover energy that might be used
for higher things.*

*The point about iron, wood, and rope not being called
strong by the wise is not just literary color. The essential point
is that things do not bind us, we bind ourselves. This is as true
of societies as it is of individuals.*

13. The wise say the fetter is strong that drags one
    down, is loose yet hard to remove; cutting
    through this, giving up the pleasure of desire, the
    indifferent one leaves the mundane.

---

*"Loose yet hard to remove." The looseness is the bit of leeway,
comfort, amusement derived from fooling around with amuse-
ments; what is hard to remove is the net of consequences that
follow upon indulgence in whatever strikes the fancy or occurs
to the mind.*

---

14. Those who are infatuated with passion fall into its
    flow as a spider does the web it has made itself.

Cutting through this, the wise go forth, unaffected, leaving all misery behind.

Spiders have ungummed walkways in their webs that enable them to get around and go about their business without getting stuck. Sometimes they stray or fall from these pathways and get trapped in their own webs. Those acts and qualities lauded by Buddha are like the walkways, those of which Buddha warns are like the gummed part of the web that acts as a trap. The web is thought, the gum is emotion.

15. Be free of the past, be free of the future, be free
    of the meantime; be transcendent. When your
    mind is completely liberated, you no longer un-
    dergo birth and old age.

---

*The **Vajracchedika Prajnaparamita-sutra**, one of the books on Wisdom Gone Beyond, says, "Past mind cannot be grasped, present mind cannot be grasped, future mind cannot be grasped." This was a favorite contemplation among some Zen Buddhist circles.*

16. Craving increases even more in the creature bur-
    dened by rumination, intensely impassioned,
    thinking this to be good; indeed, he makes his
    fetters strong.
17. One who enjoys having silenced rumination, always
    cultivating the realization that it is impure, will re-
    move, indeed cut through, the bonds of the Killer.

"Having silenced rumination" means having put a stop to useless thought, like mulling over thoughts, uselessly repeating futile thinking. It does not mean stopping all thought, only deluded thinking. The second item of the eightfold path taught by Buddha is accurate thinking. The ultimate perfection of accurate thinking is completed by silencing rumination to leave clear reflection alone.

18. One who has attained completion, is fearless, dispassionate, and unattached, has broken the stakes of existence and is in the final body.

"In the final body" means being free from compulsion to "be somebody" anymore. Having become no one and attained perfect inner peace, one reaches the end of the Lesser Journey and confronts the entryway into the Greater Journey, whereat the question of whether to be or not to be is a matter of free and independent will, not a matter of compulsion by desire to be somebody.

19. Dispassionate, unassuming, well versed in language and expression, knowing the assemblage of letters and their order, one in the final body with great insight is called a great person.

Far from being "dispassionate, unassuming, well versed in language and expression," some pseudo-Zen preachers posing as Buddhist "masters" use mistranslated meditation themes in an authoritarian setup centered on thoughtless meditation (which is, perhaps paradoxically, thought to be the purpose or goal of unnatural postures and incomprehensible stories) coupled with personal confrontations for approval or disapproval from a guru figure supposed to know all the secret "answers" to the "arcana" of the sect. The results seem to be, unfortunately, not what the **Dhammapada** *recommends here, but rather impassioned assumption-making based on self-perpetuating distortions of understanding and interpretation, fortified by intensive effort.*

20. I have overcome all, I know all, I am unaffected
    by all things. Leaving everything behind, having
    ended craving, I am freed. Having understood on
    my own, to whom should I attribute it?

Another anomalous custom developed by pseudo-Zen politicians was the practice of claiming authority for themselves by association with others. The danger in this, besides the obvious inflationary problems, was the proliferation of all sorts of nonsensical statements and actions under the banner of the supposed authority of "lineage" or institutional authority by sectarian affiliation, which naive parishioners sought vainly to rationalize, ultimately being forced to conclude that Zen is all a mystery. "QED," quoth the mad monk with a twinkle in his eye and a jingling in his jeans.

21. Giving truth surpasses all giving; the flavor of
    truth surpasses all flavors; the enjoyment of truth

surpasses all enjoyments; the destruction of craving overcomes all misery.

How pessimistic can you get?

---

22. Possessions destroy the unwise, not those who
     seek the Beyond. By craving for possessions, the
     unwise destroy others as they do themselves.

---

*"Not those who seek the Beyond." This is one of the entries into
the Greater Journey. The Zen master Dogen wrote, "To do
some good at the behest of others, to honor Buddha while
being disturbed by demons, is also awakening the mind for
enlightenment."*

*"The unwise destroy others as they do themselves." Avarice
and unscrupulousness cause wounds in the whole body of
society, not only in the individual conscience.*

*The underlying message here, again, is that the quality of
the relationship of humankind with itself and its environment
is the "essential bridge" over which we need to take control if
we are to be free to live and act in a manner that is truly
positive and creative, and not merely compulsive and wishful.*

---

23. Weeds are the bane of the fields, passion is the
     bane of humankind; so a gift to the dispassionate
     bears great fruit.
24. Weeds are the bane of the fields, hatred is the
     bane of humankind; so a gift to those free of hate
     bears great fruit.

25. Weeds are the bane of the fields, folly is the bane
    of humankind; so a gift to those free of folly
    bears great fruit.

26. Weeds are the bane of the fields, desire is the
    bane of humankind; so a gift to those free of de-
    sire bears great fruit.

----

*As noted earlier, aphorisms like 23 through 26 do not suggest
the support of armies of impudent beggars in tailored outfits,
but the support of the finer qualities in societies and individuals. It is not, furthermore, antimonastic to say this type of
saying is not an ad for monasticism as a social structure. The
point of getting at the core spiritual meaning is that the total
exercise of giving should engage the perceptions of the giver as
well as the receiver, without the emotional charge of superstitious belief. To judge people by their outwardness and what
they profess is no perceptive challenge, and so neither is it a
challenge to deceive and bilk people simply by appearing and
sounding however they have been conditioned to think is
"good" at any given time. When the inner qualities developed
in the course of the Lesser Journey develop to the point where
they are inwardly registered by others, wherever they are to be
found, then the Lesser Journey has subtly merged into the
Greater Journey, in the most harmonious possible way.*

XXV.
The Mendicant

THIS CHAPTER IS ONE OF THOSE IN WHICH
Buddha, like his Chinese contemporaries
Lao-tzu and Confucius, redefines an elemental concept of his culture. Religious wan-
derers and beggars were so common by
Buddha's time that they had virtually created
a separate caste or profession. Seeing superficial show overtake real substance, Buddha
defined the ideal of the mendicant in terms
of character and attitude rather than as an
identity or a vocation.

In the society and time of Gautama Buddha, the mendicant was already an ancient

establishment, although at that time it could be called a non-established establishment for lack of unifying principles and practices other than a need to seek beyond the parameters of the perceptions and cognitions necessary for ordinary society.

In earlier times, the mendicant was supposed to be the elder man, woman, or couple who had finished their ordinary lives and went into the forest to seek transcendental truth before passing away, surviving in the meanwhile on fruits from the trees. Some were also priests going through a period of ascetic training or vision quest.

By Buddha's time, however, expansionist Aryan militarism had driven many people of the upper, middle, *and* lower classes into mendicancy before they were really ready for such a life. As a consequence, the mendicant life became transformed into another sort of worldly career. Hence Gautama Buddha redefined the mendicant in terms of character and spiritual qualities rather than ritual usage and social status.

1. Restraint is good in the eye, good is restraint in the ear; restraint in the nose is good, good is restraint in the tongue.
2. Restraint is good in the body, good is restraint in speech. Restraint is good in thought, good is restraint in everything. The mendicant restrained in all things is freed from all misery.
3. One whose hands are controlled, whose feet are controlled, whose speech is controlled, who is supremely controlled, one who is inwardly joyful, collected, content alone, is one they call a mendicant.
4. Sweet is the speech of the mendicant who con-

trols his mouth, speaks with consideration, is not proud, and illumines the meaningful and the true.

5. A mendicant whose pleasure is truth, who delights in truth, who contemplates truth, and who follows truth, does not fall away from truth.

This critical passage underscores the point that self-mastery is a means of enabling oneself to perceive truth and live by truth. At the same time, focus on truth is essential to self-mastery in the real sense of this expression.

---

6. One should not despise what one has gotten oneself, nor envy others. A mendicant who envies others does not attain concentration.

7. Even the gods praise a mendicant who does not despise what he has gotten, even be it a little, and whose life is pure and free from laziness.

8. Whoever is free from possessiveness toward all names and forms does not sorrow because of having nothing; that is called a mendicant.

Possessiveness toward names and forms means greed for status, title, reputation, power over others, etc.

---

9. The mendicant who lives in kindness, with clear-minded faith in the teaching of the Enlightened, will go to the state of peace, the bliss where conditioning has ceased.

Scope for competitiveness and personal ambition are signs of failure in spiritual communities. Even on the Lesser Journey it is better to work in the milieu of society at large than to cloister oneself in an environment where worldly feelings are mistaken for spirituality and interpersonal tensions and contentions increase in effect, even though suppressed, through the pressurization of the cloistered environment. Besides the individual "burnout" effect this often produces, such an experience, if prolonged, can also have the negative effect of producing false impressions of Buddhism in general as excessively idealistic or incompletely effective, based on the notion that intense devotion is the same thing as accurate application, or a reasonable facsimile thereof.

10. Empty this boat, O mendicant; when it is empty, it will travel lightly. Having cut off passion and hatred, then you will go to nirvana.

Ancient Taoists also used the image of being like an "empty boat," untroubled oneself and untroublesome to others.

11. Cut off five, abandon five, rise above five; a mendicant who has surmounted the five fetters is said to have crossed over the torrent.

"Cut off five" refers to what are known as the five lower bonds, which are in the realm of desire: greed, aggression, belief in the body as real, cultic ritualism, and vacillation.

"Abandon five" refers to what are known as the five higher bonds, which are in the realm of form and the formless realm: greed in the realm of form, greed in respect to the formless, excitement, conceit, and ignorance in respect to the formless.

Many psychological manifestations ordinarily believed to be spiritual are, in this framework of understanding, still considered within the domain of bondage.

The "five fetters" here refer to passion, hatred, folly, conceit, and opinionation.

"Rise above five" refers to the five basic sense organs.

12. Meditate, O mendicant, and do not be negligent; do not let your mind be on desire. Do not swallow an iron pill through negligence; do not cry it is painful even as you burn.

13. There is no meditation for one lacking insight, no insight in one who does not meditate. One in whom are both meditation and insight is near indeed to nirvana.

Meditation without insight is not only useless, it can be harmful. It is unwise to confuse concentration, or concentration exercises (like breath counting) with meditation. Concentration and tranquilization without insight do not lead to liberation or enlightenment, and may instead magnify character flaws like greed and aggressiveness, and reduce necessary self-criticism. The early classical Zen master Baizhang said, "What the power of concentration holds leaks out and regenerates in another context, totally unawares." Nearly a thou-

sand years later, the extraordinary Japanese Zen master Bankei defined zazen *("sitting meditation") in these terms: "Harmonization with the ineffable wisdom inherent in everyone before getting involved in thinking and conceptualization is called 'meditation.' Detachment from all external objects is 'sitting.' Just sitting there with your eyes closed is not what I call zazen. Only zazen attuned to subtle knowledge is to be considered of value."*

14. To a mendicant with a calm mind who has entered an empty house, there occurs an unearthly pleasure from accurate discernment of truth.

Here, "an empty house" means this world, including one's own body, empty of delusion.

15. Whenever one comprehends the arising and passing away of the clusters, one attains a joyous happiness that is the immortality of knowers.

The "clusters" are a representation of individual being as a heap of five clusters—form, sensation, perception, combination, and consciousness. Observing these clusters as streams of energetic moments rather than fixed objects is a classical method of access to the absolute.

16. Here is the beginning in this world for an insightful mendicant: guarding the senses, contentment,
discipline conducive to liberation, association
with virtuous, pure living, and diligent friends.

*This advice on conducting oneself and associating with others
does not mention anything mysterious, occult, or requiring
acceptance on authority.*

17. Let one be friendly and well mannered; then one
will have much happiness and put an end to misery.

*Again, the constructive purpose of Buddhism emerges after the
apparently destructive practice of illusion shattering and idol
breaking.*

18. As the jasmine sheds its withered flowers, O
mendicants, you should shed passion and hatred.
19. A mendicant whose body is calm, whose speech
is calm, whose mind is calm, who is well collected, and who has spit out the bait of the
world, is said to have attained tranquillity.
20. Motivate yourself by yourself; examine yourself
by yourself. Thus self-controlled and fully conscious, you will live happily.
21. For the self is the master of the self; the self is
the resort of the self. So control yourself, as a
trader does a good horse.

Gautama Buddha did not bind people to himself in dependency relationships. _____

22. The mendicant, abounding in happiness, with clear-minded faith in the teaching of the Enlightened, will go to the state of peace, the bliss in which conditioning ceases.
23. The mendicant who applies the teaching of the Enlightened, even though young in years, lights up this world like the unclouded moon.

XXVI.
The Priestly One

THIS CHAPTER FOLLOWS ON THE MENDICANT by redefining the Brahmin, the priest of the ancient knowledge tradition. The Brahmin priesthood was the most noble caste in ancient Indian society, but confusion of the knowledge traditionally held by the priests, and the inherent weakness of a hereditary system of priestly transmission, gradually led to a weakening of the spirituality of the priesthood. As with the mendicant, therefore, Buddha redefined the concept of priestliness, based not on hereditary caste but on cultivation of specific qualities of character and behavior, here also carefully distinguishing the essence of inner reality from outward displays of piety.

Gautama Buddha abstracted and purified the definition of priestliness by basing it on character and spiritual development rather than social class. To be a Brahmin traditionally meant being born in the Brahmin caste, but Buddha's definition is not based on caste but individual self-mastery and self-purification. The Brahmin priesthood, being the noblest caste in ancient Hindu society, grew in political and economic power beyond its capacity to fulfill its ancient function of religious leadership in a proportionately evolved manner. That is, the Brahmin caste produced more offspring with specific social and personal expectations than it was able to reproduce authentically spiritual people to lead the higher life of communities. This was probably one reason why India was rife with newer speculative and contemplative schools of all sorts in the time of Gautama Buddha.

1. Cut off the flow, O priestly one; make effort, dispel desire. Knowing the extinction of conditioning, you know the uncreated.
2. In the priestly one who has gone to the goal in two principles, in the knowing one, all bonds come to an end.

"Gone to the goal in two principles" means, according to one interpretation, accomplished in "stopping and seeing" (Sanskrit samatha-vipasyana, *Pali* samatha-vipassana*), which basically means stopping delusion and seeing truth. Another level of meaning interprets the "two principles" as knowledge and action (Sanskrit* vidya-carana, *Pali* vijja-carana*), referring to the integration of perceptive and active facets of enlightenment.*

---

3. One for whom there is neither the Beyond nor
   the mundane, nor both transcendence and mundanity, one who is free from distress, unshackled,
   is the one I say is priestly.

"Neither the Beyond nor the mundane, nor both transcendence and mundanity," is a characteristic format of an entry into the Greater Journey. A typical Zen formulation of the exercise illustrated in this aphorism is the expression "Taking control of the essential bridge, do not let either the mundane or the sacred pass." This kind of entrance is commonly found in Tiantai, Zen, and other schools, through the Prajnaparamita or Wisdom Gone Beyond, the spine of the written Dharmakaya or body of Buddhist teachings.

---

4. Meditative, dispassionate, settled, accomplished,
   free from compulsion, having reached the supreme end; that is the one I say is priestly.
5. By day the sun shines, the moon illumines the
   night; the warrior shines in armor, the priestly
   one shines in meditation. But the Buddha shines
   with radiant energy day and night.

Going beyond meditation, beyond even the highest state of trance, was Buddha's own threshold of liberation. Later it came to mark the practice of those who actually followed in his footsteps.

---

6. One who wards off evil is called priestly; one who acts with equanimity is called an ascetic. When one has left behind one's own impurity, one is then called a renunciant.

7. No one should attack the priestly, but the priestly should not let loose upon one who does; woe to the killer of the priestly, and woe to one who vents anger.

8. Nothing is better for the priestly than withholding the mind from things dear. Wherever viciousness subsides, then misery ceases.

9. Whoever does no wrong physically, verbally, or mentally, who is controlled in these three respects, is one I call priestly.

10. One who has understood the truth taught by the perfectly enlightened Buddha should be honored as the priest honors the ceremonial fire.

11. One does not become priestly by matted hair, by lineage, or by birth; one in whom are reality and truth is blessed and is priestly.

12. What good is matted hair to you, idiot? What good is hide clothing? While your inward state is a tangle, you polish your exterior.

13. Clothed in used rags, so lean the veins show through the skin, meditating alone in the forest; this is the one I call priestly.

The practice of periods of abstinence to clarify unimpassioned perception was not the target of Buddha's disapproval; rather, he denounced the sentimental indulging in abstinence whether for alms from the credulous or for feelings of personal piety and self-importance.

14. I do not call someone priestly because of his origin, or his mother; such a one is called arrogant, and is possessive. The one who is nonpossessive and unattached is the one that I call priestly.

By extension, this means that pride in social origin without individual achievement is arrogance and possessiveness.

15. One who has cut through all fetters, who thus is never agitated, who has gone beyond attachment and is detached, is the one that I call priestly.
16. One who has cut the strap and the thong, and the tether and all that goes with it, one who has removed the bar, is the one that I call priestly.

The "strap, the thong, the bar, the tether, and all that goes with it" refer to the bond of egotism and the holdings of possessiveness and self-importance.

17. One who endures reproach and imprisonment even though blameless, whose power is tolerance and whose army is strength, is the one that I call priestly.

From a spiritual point of view, life on earth, life under earthly conditions, is inherently "reproach and imprisonment." Seen in that way, this passage depicts an attitude that is itself a practical way out of misery in this world.

18. One who does not anger, who is faithful to religious vows and social ethics, who is attentive, controlled, and in the last body, is the one that I call priestly.

Hearing they should not cling to desires, some people mistakenly suppose this means they should suppress desires. Since the attempted suppression is a form of clinging, the operation fails. The consequent assumption that Buddhism does not work, or is impossible to begin with, illustrates a major problem with dogmatic fixation on half-understood truths.

19. Like water on a lotus leaf, or a mustard seed on the point of a needle, one who does not cling to desires is the one that I call priestly.

20. One who knows the end of his own misery right here in this world, one who has put down his burden and is unattached, is one that I call priestly.

21. The wise one with profound insight, who knows what leads to the goal and what does not, who has reached the highest end, is one that I call priestly.

22. One who does not mix either with householders or renunciants, who does not resort to habitations, having few wants, is one that I call priestly.

Evidently Buddha didn't think that resorting to fancy ashrams would lead to inner peace.

23. One who neither kills nor causes killing, having renounced violence toward creatures mobile and stationary, is one that I call priestly.

"Stationary creatures" means beings like trees and bushes and so on.

24. One who is not hostile in the midst of the hostile, who is peaceful in the midst of those up in arms, who is unattached in the midst of the possessive, is one that I call priestly.

In Buddha's time, the Aryan conquest over ancient India was in a period of expansion, and clans of the Ksatriya caste of warriors and administrators and clans of the Brahmin caste of priests backed each other in territorial and expansionist warfare.

25. One whose passion, rage, pride, and contempt have fallen away like a mustard seed from the tip of a needle is one that I call priestly.

26. One who speaks words that are not harsh, but informative and true, by which no one is offended, is one that I call priestly.

The Tao Te Ching says, "Is it empty talk, the old saying that tact keeps you whole? When truthfulness is complete, it still resorts to this."

27. One who takes nothing in this world that is not given, be it long or short, small or large, good or bad, is one that I call priestly.
28. One who has no longing for this world or another, who is free from craving and aloof from detachment, is one that I call priestly.

Apparently many of the Hindu yogis were trapped by longing for other worlds. Abandoning otherworldly longings is a hallmark of Buddhist teaching, practice, and enlightenment.

29. One who has no dependence, freed from doubt through perfect knowledge, who has reached immersion in the ambrosia of immortality, is one that I call priestly.
30. One who has passed beyond both virtue and sin in this world, sorrowless, dispassionate, pure, is one that I call priestly.

To pass beyond virtue does not mean to be inactive, but to pass beyond the state of expecting and demanding to be rewarded for virtue. This passing beyond is one of the entrances, or transition points, into the Greater Journey. The Taoist Huainan Masters say, "Making a big deal out of doing good is like making a big deal out of doing wrong, insofar as it is not near the Way."

_____

31. Stainless and pure as the moon, serene and un-ruffled, one in whom the occurrence of craving has ceased is one that I call priestly.

32. One who has gone beyond this muddy road, this hard-going routine delusion, the meditative one who has crossed over, transcended, free from lust, without a doubt, ungrasping, perfectly se-rene, is one that I call priestly.

33. One who goes forth unsheltered, having given up longing in this world, one in whom the occur-rence of longing has ceased, is one that I call priestly.

34. One who goes forth unsheltered, having given up all craving in this world, one in whom the occur-rence of craving has ceased, is one that I call priestly.

_____

"Unsheltered," in the spiritual sense, means having resort to no illusions, being open to reality, exposed to truth.

_____

35. One who is free of all entanglement, having given up entanglement in the human and gone

beyond entanglement in the divine, is one that I call priestly.

36. The hero who has overcome all the world, having given up pleasure and displeasure, calm and unattached, is one that I call priestly.

"Having given up pleasure and displeasure" means living by free will, by the power of purpose, not being compelled, with the help of the vagaries of circumstances, simply by preoccupation with seeking pleasure and avoiding displeasure just for one's own personal comfort.

---

37. One who knows the perishing and arising of beings everywhere, without fixation, gone the right way, awakened, is one that I call priestly.

To "know the perishing and arising of beings" means to be aware of the coexistence of transitoriness and persistence of habit, to know that everything passes while also knowing how things get started.

---

38. One whose path is unknown to gods, cherubim, or human beings, the worthy in whom compulsions have ended, is one that I call priestly.

Classical Zen texts emphasize the path that "no celestial beings can see to strew flowers upon, and no demons or outsiders can see to spy upon."

39. One for whom there is nothing at all before, af-
    ter, or in the meanwhile, who has nothing and
    clings to nothing, is one that I call priestly.

The **Vajracchedika Prajnaparamita-sutra** *says, "Past mind cannot be grasped, present mind cannot be grasped, future mind cannot be grasped." Because this is an exercise in mental posture as well as a metaphysical truth, it has to be tried to be appreciated.*

---

40. The noble one, the excellent one, the valiant
    one, the great seer, the victorious one, the pas-
    sionless one, the purified one, the awakened one,
    is one that I call priestly.
41. One who knows former abodes, and sees paradise
    and hell, the sage established in higher knowledge
    who has reached the end of birth, the one who
    has accomplished all that is to be accomplished, is
    one that I call priestly.

Knowledge of former abodes, a capacity normally attributed to Buddhas and Buddhist saints, means insight into the inventory of one's own experiences and those of others, and into the way in which we have experienced our experiences and how we have digested them, or how we have suffered from indigestion.

This is not the end of the Dhammapada. The Dhammapada is a wheel, not a line. Now go back to the "beginning."

About the Translator

Thomas Cleary has studied Zen koans for thirty years, and has long been acknowledged worldwide as a master translator of Zen texts. His acclaimed translations of Buddhist and Taoist classics, renowned for their unusual lucidity, have been adopted as international standards for retranslation into French, Dutch, German, Italian, Portuguese, Spanish, and Turkish.

The new accessibility of Eastern ideas through Dr. Cleary's expert translations has extended their audience beyond the cultural fringes of Western civilization to the vanguard of modern thinking in science, education, business, and diplomacy.